# AN INTRODUCTION
# TO THE STUDY OF
# HISTORY

# AN INTRODUCTION
# TO THE STUDY OF
# HISTORY

BY

V. H. GALBRAITH

LONDON
C. A. WATTS & CO., LTD.

*First published* 1964

©

C. A. WATTS & CO. LTD
1964

PRINTED IN GREAT BRITAIN BY
BUTLER AND TANNER LTD, FROME AND LONDON
36/429

# TO THE READER

I COMMEND this book to the Reader in the spirit of King James's instructions regarding Guy Fawkes (Plate VI below). 'The gentler tortours are to be first usid unto him *et sic per gradus ad ima tenditur.*[1] And so god speede youre goode worke.' Part I deals with the grammar of the subject which is best approached, with the help of textbooks, by a preliminary canter over as wide a field as possible. A second stage is reached in Part II when the textbooks are harnessed to the original documents which are their sources. In the third part the student is assumed to be at least beginning to think his own history and even occasionally to write it.

The first part reproduces (with some changes) a pamphlet called *The Historian at Work*. This was written for the British Broadcasting Corporation, to whom my thanks are due for kind permission to reprint it. Though the mistakes and omissions are all my own, I have to acknowledge gratefully the help of many expert friends in its composition. More especially, on newspapers and coins, I am indebted to Mr Hanson of the Bodleian Library and to Dr Sutherland and Mr A. Thompson of the Ashmolean Museum. To Miss Jean Rowntree, Head of Further Education Unit, B.B.C., I am grateful for some of its material, as well as for helpful criticism throughout. The second part, which reprints an inaugural lecture given at Edinburgh twenty-five years ago, tries to express what seems to me to matter most in the study of history, and re-echoes much of Part I which was in fact distilled from

[1] And so by stages to the most extreme.

it. Part III attempts to convey some understanding of that much-abused word Research. Not everyone who reads the first part will want to bother with Part II; while very few, I imagine, will persevere so far as to read the long concluding section. A lifetime of teaching has undermined my early faith in the possibility of telling other people how to research, or how, having researched, to put results into print. The longer one studies history, the harder it gets to arrive at results which even the author, let alone the reader, can decently consider to be the truth. In this state of mind, I thought it best simply to print, as an example to be shot down by all who read it, my examination of a well-worn problem with a few comments on the process, and the results obtained. Large morals could be drawn from Part III, but I shall have succeeded in my aim if this inquiry—typical of many scores with which the historian is daily faced—suggests how shaky are the foundations sustaining the confident narratives we write, and how endless is the work that still remains to be done. Historical study to many of us is an expanding revelation whose ever-increasing fascination only deepens the conviction that one is still a beginner.

To Mr T. M. Schuller, Sir Roger Mynors and to my daughter Mary I am variously indebted for help in bringing this little book to birth.

V. H. G.

*Oxford, 1963*

# CONTENTS

## ACKNOWLEDGMENTS

Permission to reproduce material for the Plates is gratefully acknowledged to the following:

Aerofilms and Aero Pictorial Ltd. (Plate XIV); the Bodleian Library, Oxford (Plate III); the Trustees of the British Museum (Plates IV, V, VII, XII); the Clarendon Press, Oxford (Plates VIII, XX); Wm. Collins Sons & Co. Ltd. (Plate XIX); the Controller, Her Majesty's Stationery Office (Plates VI, IX, X, XI); the Mansell Collection (Plates XVI, XVII); the Trustees of the National Gallery, London (Plate XVIII); the South Shields Public Libraries and Museums Committee (Plate II); J. K. St Joseph, Esq. (Plate XV); *The Times* (Plate XIII).

# LIST OF ILLUSTRATIONS

*(between pp. 72 and 73)*

# PART I

# The Historian at Work

# 1

## THE NATURE OF HISTORY AND OF HISTORICAL EVIDENCE

WHAT is history? We require a definition, and for want of a better, let us take Marc Bloch's, that history is the science of men in time. Every word of it so manifestly begs a question that we must try to explain our terms in detail. By science we mean a body of knowledge that seeks to tell the truth, the whole truth and nothing but the truth. This is a task for a dedicated man, yet for those who are born for it, it can and should be great fun. But the research it entails has its own rules, which we call historical method, and these have to be learned. It may even be that no one yet fully understands them, for the study of history as pursued today is quite recent—not much more than a century old.

In describing history as a science and thus aligning ourselves with the school of Ranke and J. B. Bury, we are doing no more than stating an ideal, to which we must cling, however unattainable in practice. And this clears up at least two common misunderstandings. The first of these is the confusion of history with literature. Between the two there is no essential connexion, however much and long they have been associated. By all means write like Macaulay and Gibbon—if you can—but however one writes and whatever one writes about, the basic aim should be to arrive at the bare truth. Truth and rhetoric are bad bedfellows. This needs to be said, since all historical writing is to some degree a matter of creative imagination, and the

3

greater the writer the more apt he is to be carried away. This then is not a tract for budding authors, for no one can tell another how to write history, though, as I have said, there are some really rigid rules for studying it. Clio, once a Muse, is now more commonly seen, with a reader's ticket, verifying her references at the Public Record Office.

The second has to do with what we used to call our prejudices, but is today euphemistically labelled as 'bias'. It is now commonly, and truly, said that the writing of objective history is impossible; that its only completely impartial exponent is the Recording Angel; and that therefore 'bias' is all right so long as you come clean about it. This soothing doctrine enables us still to cling to our Gibbon and Macaulay, but it is none the less unacceptable, for it means that the historian, like the barrister, is no more than the advocate and defender of one side or the other. As an ideal it simply won't do, for it implies a failure of understanding on the part of the author. If we could perfectly understand the past, our prejudices—race, religion, nationalism, politics—which are our limitations, would be swallowed up and disappear in perfect human sympathy, pity and wonder. 'Many are the marvels and none so marvellous as man.' Of course, we are all prejudiced, but we can and should struggle with our prejudices, and, as it were, fall over backwards to overcome them. In this heroic and perhaps unavailing attempt lies the salutary discipline of historical study. In no other study is mere cleverness at a greater discount and single-minded devotion at a higher premium.

History then is a science, the science of men. In studying history we are finding out about ourselves, and in the last resort the natural sciences and even mathematics have the same final end. But these, of course, by reason of their immediate subject matter are more objective, for, despite the claims of the psychologists to split personality, we have not so far learned to treat men like atoms. For us they are still individuals, all different, and the economic man, for example, exists only in the textbooks of political economists. The real trouble about history as the science of men is that its scope is entirely undefined. There can be a history of anything and of everything, and in this sense history is a method of arriving at truth rather than a subject in itself. It is just one way of explaining ourselves to ourselves.

Finally, history is the science of men in time. This is the real crux of the matter, for it is at once history's fundamental limitation and its life blood. If time were to stand still history would soon cease, once the existing evidence was fully sifted. For time means change, and as we have no warrant for thinking that there is anything that does not suffer from inexorable change and final oblivion, it means that history must be rewritten for each succeeding generation. For each generation sees things rather differently from the preceding one, and asks new questions. Few parents can have failed to notice that their children do not see eye to eye with themselves, and this process, interminably repeated, means that the nature and aims of history also change. It is often said that you have one constant, since human nature remains the same. This is nonsense. For men are moulded by their ever-changing environment. Nor can we escape from this dilemma by limiting our history to a simple narration of events. At every step the historian is required to make moral judgments, to label men 'good' or 'bad'. These like everything else vary from age to age, and the historian can do no more than strive to apply the best standards, not of his own time, but of the period with which he is concerned.

Another and very practical difficulty, well explained by

Herbert Butterfield's *Whig Interpretation of History*, is posed by time. When we study the origins of states and institutions, we are in the unhappy position of knowing the result of the process we are examining, and thereby tempted to think that it was implicit in its beginnings. Here it is only necessary to point out that this limited determinism was much increased by the publication of Darwin's *Origin of Species* (1859). 'The roots of the present', wrote Bishop Stubbs, borrowing the metaphor of evolution and natural selection, 'lie deep in the past', and armed by this analogy our native historians have come near to describing our modern parliamentary constitution as the natural and inevitable outcome of free Teutons imported from the forests of Germany more than a thousand years ago! And this in turn raises the question: Are there then no accidents in history? Is it just all cause and effect, by which everything turned out for the best in the best of all possible worlds, in the shape of nineteenth-century England? On these unanswerable questions there is and always will be endless debate 'about it and about', but they have no place in a short account of the *Historian at Work*. For him it is enough that his very curiosity has been shaped by his upbringing and that the questions to which he seeks the answers should at best be worded rather differently from those of his predecessors. He thus brings a new, as well as a fresh mind to his work, intent to re-think the thoughts of the men in his chosen period, and alive to the danger of anachronism.

The starting point of all inquiry is our immediate environment—the town, the street, the very house in which we live and the family to which we belong. All these are physical survivals of the past, inviting investigation and linking us with our forefathers. We thus start from the known, and all our histories are no more than hypotheses to explain how the world around us came to be what it is. Every parish church, with its memorials and furnishings is a museum: the very shapes of our fields, and our tortuous, twisting roads are full of meaning if they can be read aright. Aerial photography has brought to light lost villages, and prehistoric earthworks by the thousand. Coins, weapons, armour and the implements of husbandry survive in plenty and have been made the subject of specialist inquiry. The historian can thus turn for help to architecture, maps, numismatics, heraldry, painting and portraiture, art —each of them a study in its own right.

Visual studies apart, the past lives on in local and central government, in law and philology, and in the ceremonies of church, state, towns and our universities. The modern parliament by which we are ruled exercises the delegated authority of a sovereign queen. Domesday Book (1086) is still copied and quoted in the law courts, and every Secretary of State still takes office by the receipt of the queen's signet. The coronation service is more than a thousand years old, and Magna Carta is still a vital part of legal process. The Treasury is as old as monarchy itself, and the office of Lord Chancellor hardly less venerable. Terms, titles and ceremonies remain unchanged, even when the institutions to which they refer have for the most part completely altered their character. Nevertheless the very survival of the outward forms bears witness to the unbroken continuity of English history, and the unshakable conservatism of its people. They have never been separated from their past by revolution, and the reason why the study of history is less advanced in this country than in Germany is largely because we have never had to re-discover our past. In England we live our history more than we study it, or perhaps we just take it for granted. Yet the plain man is acutely aware that things aren't what they used to be and that times have changed.

From this low-level interest in the past rises the earliest and most primitive kind of history—tradition. Indeed, if we go back far enough there is no other form. Domesday Book is full of it, and the first use of the sworn jury in England was to collect the testimony of living men regarding past events. For tradition the modern historian has more respect in early times than the present, when they tend to regard it as little more than old wives' tales. Much of the early history of Rome, and, in fact, of all countries, is little more than legend later committed to writing, and our Victorian grandfathers had a touching faith in the 'unfagged memory' of early man to transmit accurately an oral record. Today we bring to our written records a sterner criticism which is the foundation of modern research.

We turn then to the historian's materials, limiting the discussion—for convenience—to British history, and defining history as the record of those centuries for which there is written evidence, however partial and inadequate: that is, from the Roman occupation to the present day. For this period of nearly two thousand years, the historian is primarily concerned with the criticism of written documents, though substantially assisted, as we shall see, by other techniques.

The further we go back, of course, the fewer the documents. Thus, for Roman times digging is still more rewarding than reading. Thenceforward we have a growing trickle of written evidence, still occasional, casual and uneven in value as evidence, making the history of many aspects of these early times virtually impossible. But at the very outset of the thirteenth century, with the beginnings of the official archives preserved in the Public Record Office, we pass from a customary and largely oral society to an age of record, which extends unbroken to the present day. With the thirteenth century the historian is, so to speak, in a new world. There is far more material: there is greater certainty, or at least less uncertainty, and in many fields, notably in Economics, there is almost endless scope for future inquiry.

One other landmark in the broadening stream of evidence is marked by the supersession of Latin by English as the normal language for documents in the sixteenth century. The use of the vernacular led to a vast increase of informal letters, diaries and so on. These bring us nearer to the live thoughts of men than was possible when they were couched in a dead language, and it is no accident that the first truly modern and adequate biography of an English king is A. F. Pollard's *Henry VIII*.

Lastly, from the late eighteenth century onwards the possible sources of history increase in geometrical proportion until the present day when they are so vast as to defy exhaustive historical criticism. A few volumes for example are enough for all the statutes of Parliament enacted in the first four centuries of its existence, while for the two remaining centuries the volumes fill the whole length of a large room. Similarly the records of the first great war, if preserved in their entirety, would, it was calculated, have filled the Crystal Palace.

This cursory survey of the evidence available for modern history suggests the practical conclusion that the historian who is anxious to give significant answers to significant questions will do well to avoid the remoter past and the

B

near present, though of the two the latter alternative is, perhaps, preferable. In the Middle Ages as in the classical period you are most happy when, as so often, you depend upon a single testimony. The trouble begins when you have several documents which disagree. Professor Le Patourel provides a classic instance of this difficulty in his recent discussion of the conflicting dates assigned to the famous plea at Penenden Heath, near Maidstone, when archbishop Lanfranc complained of encroachments upon his lands in Kent. Although there are three contemporary accounts, it is possible to quote at least one modern historian in favour of each year from 1070 to 1077, and Professor Le Patourel concludes that the conflict cannot be resolved, and seems unlikely ever to be resolved in the future.

There are, fortunately, printed guides to the sources, by means of which the historian can pick his way across the centuries. For the Middle Ages we have Charles Gross' *Sources and Literature of English History to about 1485*, and for more modern times others covering shorter periods, such as Conyers Read's *Bibliography of British History 1485–1603*. These books, though they begin to go out of date from the day they are published, are indispensable aids, and it is almost frightening to realise that similar works exist for every civilised country. The latter, too, are a warning of the danger of confining our attention, even in a short pamphlet, to English history from Roman times. The historian of English government cannot ignore that of neighbouring countries, and the historian of our towns must familiarise himself with civic development in at least western Europe. He will moreover, if he is wise, make some comparative study of the city state of the ancient world.

For the purposes of historical criticism, the written

sources of history are traditionally divided into two classes—chronicles and records. Chronicles are taken to include the whole of the literary sources, works, that is, written for posterity, and records all documents arising in the way of administration and business, and thus intended primarily for contemporary use.

Chronicles and histories until fairly recent times were the chief and often the only sources employed by the historian. By them we can best hope to understand the thoughts and mental attitudes of earlier times. Their authors say what they think about men and events, and in using them we have always to allow for their personal feeling. We are for instance much better informed throughout the entire Middle Ages about the affairs of the Church than of the State, simply because literacy was a clerical monopoly. It follows that when, as happened so often, Church and State were at loggerheads, we must allow for clerical bias, especially as regards the character and motives of individuals. The truth about William Rufus, King John and Frederick II of Germany—to take three notorious examples—is today hardly discoverable in the violently partisan contemporary chronicles. As late even as the seventeenth century we have not yet found a satisfactory middle way between the Roundhead and Cavalier points of view, and the same is true of the Chartist movement in the nineteenth century. On the other hand it is not so nice a problem to hold the balance between the Whigs and the Tories in the eighteenth and nineteenth centuries, since, for all their differences, both sides had much in common. But in all periods the literary sources require careful scrutiny, and we need to know everything possible about their authors to allow for personal distortion.

Records and archives as they are now called, which till a

century ago were mere subsidiaries of the literary sources, are becoming more and more important in historical research. Every government and administration, every business and every individual is in the nature of things compelled to amass archives. They are a function of all administration, public and private, and their possibilities as historical evidence have been increasingly recognised in the twentieth century. Their sovereign advantage as material is held to lie in the fact that their compilers had no thought of the future. They seemed therefore to afford a vast store-house of facts, free from bias and so incontrovertible. In the nineteenth century great sums of money were spent by governments in arranging, classifying and publishing their national archives. Their example was followed by the papacy, and in England today the greatest single centre of research is the Public Record Office in Chancery Lane founded in 1838.

Thus in the nineteenth century the study of history was wholly transformed. Hitherto the mere hobby of antiquaries, it became a serious study, which at the universities gave rise to a large class of professional historians and ended the monopoly of the Latin and Greek classics as the normal form of a liberal education. This movement was closely bound up with a growing preference for records, rather than chronicles and histories, as the basic materials for study. More and more scholars realised that, though history does not repeat itself, historians repeated one another: that histories were essentially put together from earlier writers: that they are often full of gross mis-statements of simple facts, swayed by personal prejudice: and that their evidence was nearly always to some degree suspect. Records contrariwise were seen to be 'original' documents of exact (and contemporary) date and provenance: and scholars, like Lord Acton (1834-1902), had a vision of a new, scientific history which would attain to ultimate truth.

In the last generation this vision slowly faded out as experience showed that records, no less than the literary sources, are generally compiled from other documents, often unknown to us and that they rarely tell the whole truth. Records, in fact, can no more be taken at their face value than chronicles. Domesday Book, for example, is no original document, but a condensed summary of a complicated series of semi-judicial proceedings, and, moreover, full of errors. Magna Carta, issued as the free grant of King John to his subjects, was in fact a treaty between the king and his barons, which the king at least never meant to observe. Even the routine government activities, such as the Inquisitions *post mortem* into the property of deceased tenants-in-chief, were more than slightly 'bogus'. In form these documents were the declarations of a sworn jury but in fact they can only have been made by the steward of the dead man in consultation with the king's escheator. The facts regarding the deposition of Richard II in 1399 were obscured by a too simple reliance upon the 'official' *Rolls of Parliament*, which at this moment are a partisan compilation intended to justify his successor, Henry IV.

Thus, in using records as evidence, we have to subject them to a sensitive criticism which seeks to discover the materials behind them and the impression which they were intended to produce. Indeed, speaking very roughly, it will be found that most records—from Acts of Parliament to balance sheets of public companies and diplomatic notes— have some sort of bias of their own, and seek to conceal the truth or a part of it. The result of the vast extension of research by the use of official documents has thus been to make the writing of history more difficult but very much more exciting. A prudent man will still pay equal attention to both sorts of evidence. Both require to be handled with skill, and each has its own dangers. We still cannot write history from records alone, which disguise the feelings and thoughts both of their makers and their time. Still less can we put our sole trust in histories and chronicles which, though rarely quite wrong, are never quite right. The two forms of evidence, which at first sight often conflict, have somehow to be reconciled by the historian.

The historian's chief concern is, then, with the original and contemporary sources. Even if these are already in print, their texts require scrutiny. More often they are still in manuscript and have to be deciphered. Handwriting, like all the arts, has a long history, and its development has been intensively studied under the name of Palaeography. By handwriting alone we can date a manuscript within half a century or so, and in early periods so great are the local variations that we can generally learn something of a document's *provenance* or place of origin. It is also the key to modern printing, by which it has been slowly superseded. No less necessary is knowledge of the various systems of chronology or measurements of time. This work for the most part has already been done and is readily available in handbooks. The same is true of seals by which, owing to the general illiteracy, all important documents were authenticated until a relatively recent period. These special studies require in turn a working acquaintance with administrative history, which traces the development of the various and often separate departments of government.

And so, in ever-widening circles the historian is led on to the study of other branches of knowledge such as geography, architecture, archaeology, economics and psychology, as he realises that there is scarcely any branch of inquiry which may not be used to throw light on the past. In the past half-century his work has been further stimulated by new techniques such as aerial photography, which has laid bare the sites of Celtic fields, Roman towns and lost villages: by the publications of the Place-Name Society, so valuable for the earliest village settlements in England: and by the cheap production of microfilms and photostats, which have revolutionised the study of handwriting. Such new techniques moreover are certain to increase as the historian of the future learns to handle statistics, to measure the growth of population (demography), to use computers and photogrammetry and to date in laboratories the very materials of archaeology.

There remains to be mentioned one other master influence upon the development of historical criticism, viz. forgery. At every stage in the evolution of historical science, forgery has played an important part. The word has an ugly ring today, but in earlier times only two sorts of forgery brought heavy penalties—forgery of the king's seal or of the coinage. Mere literary forgery was no more than the clergyman's peccadillo and its heyday was the eleventh and twelfth centuries when, in a largely oral and customary society, written documents were still something of a novelty. For centuries the supremacy of the archbishopric of Canterbury over that of York rested comfortably upon a series of forged papal letters or bulls, although the forgery was discovered at Rome in 1123 by the clever papal officials. The monks, we are told, explained that the seals of the 'original' bulls were perished or lost: whereupon some of the Roman officials 'smiled, others wrinkled their noses, others broke forth into laughter, and said that it was very odd that the lead (of the seals) was perished or lost and that the parchment was preserved!' But though York had the better of the argument, the supremacy of Canterbury went on undisturbed. For there was not as yet any 'public opinion' which condemned forgery. In the following century, the enlightened Papal court introduced ingenious devices in their bulls by which forgery could be detected; and in the fifteenth century some long-standing forgeries like the Donation of Constantine were exposed. But it was not till the year 1681 that the serious criticism of historical documents was raised to the level of a science by the publication of Jean Mabillon's *De re diplomatica*. Mabillon was a Benedictine monk, and his object—brilliantly achieved— was to refute a Jesuit pamphlet which had questioned the authenticity of the early charters of the royal abbey of St Denis. In this great book, the author traced in detail across the centuries the development of handwriting, and of the structure of documents, and so began the separation of genuine from spurious charters. Thenceforward slowly emerged the twin sciences of palaeography and diplomatic which are taught today in our universities.

Meanwhile sporadic forgeries both of charters and of literary works have continued. In 1697, an eminent classical scholar, Richard Bentley, proved the 'Letters of Phalarys' to be forgeries, but the *De situ Britanniae* (1757), an impudent forgery purporting to describe Roman Britain, imposed upon the learned world for more than a century, until finally exposed by J. E. B. Mayor. In our own day many scholars were induced—for a time—to believe in the 'discovery' of the lost books of Livy. Nor, of course, is forgery confined to documents. The 'Glozel' pottery, and the 'Piltdown Man' (*Eoanthropus dawsoni*) are enough to remind us of the almost unfathomable credulity of mankind, and no doubt there are other forgeries which still await discovery.

The study of history, then, imposes rigorous rules, as well as a self-discipline upon those who pursue it. In this brief sketch greater emphasis has been laid upon the distant past than the near present, simply because English history has for nearly 1,000 years been more free from cataclysmic revolution and desolating invasion than its neighbours. In no other country do existing political and social institutions retain so many and so strong links with the past. The two tragic wars of the twentieth century have, by quickening the pace of change, rather obscured and certainly weakened this continuity, which has none the less moulded our national habits of thought and feeling.

The study of what is called contemporary history presents new problems of historical criticism even more insuperable than those of the past; and an adequate criticism for dealing with it has still to be evolved. The sheer immensity of the sources, the influence of world-wide propaganda, the material power of autocratic governments and the passionate feeling attaching to living issues make greater demands than ever before upon the responsible historian. All this suggests the paradoxical conclusion that while we know more about the contemporary world than about earlier periods, its history has less hope of being objective than that of, say, a century ago.

The historical criticism outlined above slowly evolved from the study of antiquity and the Middle Ages. For these remote periods it has narrowed the area of disagreement among historians, and thereby made historical study more objective. Even in the sixteenth and early seventeenth centuries it still provides the means for a balanced judgment

of events, though the outlook of the historians of this age
has been deeply affected by the new autocracies and the
growing secularism of the twentieth century. To contemporary influences of this kind, rather than to any advance
in method, are due new and conflicting interpretations
both of politics and of personalities like Henry VIII, Straf-
ford, and Oliver Cromwell.

As we approach the end of the seventeenth century the
old approach becomes less valid, owing to the rapid pro-
liferation of the sources and their changing character. The
possibilities of more detailed and more personal knowledge
of events grows greater with the increase of memoirs,
tracts, letters and, above all, newspapers; and as we enter
the nineteenth century we begin to lose the perspective
afforded by distance from events. By the middle of that
century the historian's difficulty is not so much one of
gathering information, as of sifting the conflicting evidence
of almost overwhelming sources. A more empirical approach becomes necessary and the differences between
historians become more irreconcilable: so that when at
last we reach the contemporary age, history, too often,
becomes mere politics, and too often the servant of conflicting ideologies. But not always. Method, however
important, is no more than a tool; and over two thousand
years ago Thucydides, a retired general, wrote an account
of the Peloponnesian War (*his* war), which many good
judges have held to be the greatest *History* ever written.

It is in near-contemporary times that interest chiefly lies
today and a vast historical literature pours from the presses.
A distinguished living historian[1] of the nineteenth century—
well grounded in the historical criticism of earlier periods—
has described in detail his procedure in adapting the old
criticism to the new material, and thereby drawn a fascinat-

ing picture of the modern historian at work. Taking as his thesis the French revolution of 1848, Sir Llewellyn Woodward suggests that there are four types of historical question to be asked: 1. What happened? 2. Why did it happen? 3. Why did it happen in such and such a way, and not otherwise? 4. What is the meaning or value of its happening?

So detailed a probe of the past is made possible by the abundance of information, and the appearance of new techniques such as photography and shorthand. To answer his questions the historian is driven to a new classification of his material into 1. Documents of state; 'official' sources of diplomatic history, and 2. Memoirs, letters, newspapers and other material. Documents of state and public acts are still the most reliable forms of historical authority if only because their bias and their assumptions can be better checked than before by other evidence. For instance one of the protocols of the Congress of Berlin notes the absence of the chief Russian plenipotentiary, Prince Gortchakoff, from an important session owing to 'illness'. An eyewitness however noticed in his diary that the sick man spent the period eating strawberries on the balcony of his hotel! But if documents of state are still the most reliable sources, it is from documents in the second category that the amazing wealth of detail is chiefly derived. Memoirs, letters, diaries, autobiographies—each of these, however much they over-lap—have their special value and dangers, and newspapers have a far greater importance than ever before. Their influ-ence was enormous, and men like Delane, the editor of *The Times* moving in the highest society, had constant access to confidential information. Yet they need care-ful handling, since 'the element of distance is wanting: there is no horizon'. 'Great events,' we are told, 'like great emotions, must be remembered in tranquillity, if their record is to be more than lyrical': and this limitation applies with particular force to the daily press.

That there should be great differences in the interpretation of evidence at once so voluminous and so tricky to use, is only to be expected. The nearer we approach to the present the greater the demands not only upon sympathy and understanding but also upon mental subtlety in the sifting of so much detailed, but often doubtful evidence.

What of the future? Historical method, as sketched above, was evolved (chiefly in Germany) in the course of the nineteenth century. Natural science was then in its infancy, while the classics and theology were steadily losing ground. History was more and more felt to be the subject of the future, and by the middle of the century, 'it had established', writes Professor Southern[2], 'the same kind of mysterious power over men's minds that science has gained in our own day'. In this climate of opinion scholars turned to history, and, in particular, to constitutional history. They were fascinated by the conception of our parliamentary constitution—then at the height of its reputation —as the inevitable product of two thousand years of evolution: and this special angle of approach gave a certain unity to their researches. The greatest name in the modern period was Macaulay; and in the medieval bishop Stubbs; and the gathering force of a succession of workers was felt in both fields. A single example will suffice. The enigmatic figure of Oliver Cromwell stands at the very heart of the 'century of Revolution'. His fame was quickly effaced by the Restoration in 1660. Thenceforth he was universally accepted as half fanatic, half hypocrite and 'guilty of his country's blood' until the publication of his *Letters and Speeches* by Thomas Carlyle in 1845: 'Not a man of falsehood', said Carlyle, 'but a man of truth'; and this instinctive discovery was slowly substantiated by the successive labours of S. R. Gardiner, James Gairdner and others, culminating in Sir Charles Firth's *Oliver Cromwell* (1900).

For a moment Firth seemed to be the 'last word'. But the thoughts of men 'are never at a stand'. Already by the turn of the century the impulse given by constitutional history was nearly exhausted, and the fashion of historians turning to a more economic approach.

Today, a new generation, the product of two world wars, finds no satisfaction in Victorian history. More than Cromwell has gone by the board; and the men and women are perhaps already born to whom it will fall to rewrite the huge, co-operative *Oxford History of England*, now barely completed.

# 2

## TECHNIQUES AND AUXILIARY SCIENCES

PALAEOGRAPHY

For the historian working on any period later than the sixteenth century, the study of palaeography involves little more than a certain low cunning—quickly gained by practice—in deciphering bad writing. There were still writing masters and scriveners, and even an outstanding script, called Secretary hand; but as an art handwriting, having been ousted by printing, was out at elbow and down at heel. Even so, the most modern researcher needs to know that our alphabet is that of imperial Rome; that our capital letters have remained unchanged for two thousand years, and that the ordinary print of a modern newspaper goes back to the writing of the Italian humanists of the fifteenth century, who revived the beautiful Caroline minuscule of the ninth century. This script was used by the early printers of the fifteenth and sixteenth centuries, and so saved from either development or deterioration. In Germany, the home of printing, the unreformed Gothic script was used as their model and has persisted there to the present century.

For the thousand years before the invention of printing, palaeography is a much more valuable tool, and requires more serious study. In this period handwriting was one of the fine arts, governed by its own rules, reflecting the slowly changing civilisation of which its best manuscripts —miracles of calligraphy—are now precious, physical survivals. For most of the period, the language of manuscripts was Latin, though in England there was a special script for books in the vernacular, and from the twelfth century a growing number of Anglo-Norman manuscripts. In that illiterate age the practice of writing was virtually confined to the Church, that is to educated ecclesiastics—clerks, monks and notaries. The material used was sheepskin, and the pen was a quill. From about the fourteenth century, paper, a much inferior medium, came into use, and gradually superseded sheepskin. The great legacy of this period to the modern world was the simple and beautiful Caroline minuscule, which gradually took the place of the earlier majuscule hands—rustic capitals, uncials and half-uncials. From the ninth to the twelfth century this was the reigning script, until the sudden change to Gothic hand of the thirteenth century. By this time writing was divided into two branches: Text or Bookhand used for works of lasting importance, and Court Hand or cursive which, in turn, was written in either a set (copybook) hand, or more freely according to personal idiosyncrasies. To save labour the scribes had long since perfected an elaborate system of abbreviations, the study of which is valuable both for dating manuscripts and determining their provenance.

By their script, as well as by their abbreviations and similar technicalities, manuscripts can be safely dated within half a century or so, in a manner parallel with that used for dating churches, castles and cathedrals. For more exact dating the historian must turn to the internal evidence afforded by his text, or by allied documents. Plates IV and V, for example, show two hands in a Dominican service book, which were long thought to be nearly contemporary, until internal evidence showed that a full century divides them. In the later Middle Ages, the chief departments of the central government—the Chancery, the Exchequer, and the courts of law—each evolved distinctive hands of their own, by which their products can be recognised at a glance. The monastic houses, whose books were rudely dispersed at the Dissolution (1536–9) also developed characteristic hands by which, together with the press-marks and medieval catalogues, it is possible to reconstruct their libraries. We are fortunate, too, in possessing autograph manuscripts of our medieval historians, such as William of Malmesbury in the twelfth century, and Matthew Paris—the most famous of them all (plate XII)— in the thirteenth century. His handwriting, about which there was much controversy, has lately been accurately identified by Mr Vaughan; and in the fine manuscripts of his history preserved in the British Museum and at Corpus Christi College, Cambridge, we can, as it were, watch him at work, ever amending and adding to his original text.

Autograph manuscripts, however, are the exception; and we are apt to forget how much time was spent by medieval scribes in merely multiplying copies of existing books and 'glossing' them with marginal commentaries; or, in Anglo-Saxon times, by adding interlinear translations. The modern editor of one of these must collate the best copies of his author, noting their various readings, and endeavouring in this way to get back, so far as it is possible, to the author's original. Great skill has been developed in this work of textual criticism, in which one must always be on the look-out for words or even whole sentences omitted by a scribe who had nodded over his task. This laborious editorial work has lately been transformed by photography, so that by microfilms and projectors the scholar can in effect assemble a number of manuscripts in one place, often with striking results. In a forthcoming new edition of

Richard of Devizes' chronicle, for example, it was discovered that only one of the two surviving manuscripts was written by the author. Yet three highly competent, nineteenth-century editors, lacking photographs, had pronounced both manuscripts to be his.

## DIPLOMATIC AND CHRONOLOGY

The science of Diplomatic is concerned with the criticism of official or business documents, such as rolls and accounts: and more especially with charters, royal and private. In the nineteenth century continental scholars, like Von Sickel, Harry Bresslau and Leopold Delisle examined in minute detail the structure, dating, sealing and legal force of charters and papal bulls. Their researches, covering the whole Middle Ages, were conveniently summarised in A. Giry's *Manuel de diplomatique* (1894). There is no English handbook—a striking fact, since no other country is so rich in diplomatic sources. Since its beginnings in Mabillon's *De re diplomatica* diplomatic has been closely connected with the discovery of forgery, and the student of diplomatic endeavours by the study of surviving originals to lay down rules for distinguishing between the true and the false. From such originals we can, for example, fix the moment at which Henry II first began to style himself King *by the Grace of God* (*dei gratia*) and distinguish between the seven or eight great seals of Edward III. The drafting and phraseology of charters also slowly change from reign to reign; and by such criteria, together with that of handwriting, a very precise criticism is applied to doubtful documents. The diplomatic approach, so valuable for classical and medieval history, loses much of its validity as other sources of information increase, and efforts to extend

c

its sphere into the modern period have had only a moderate success.

Chronology is, of course, the very bedrock of history; and medieval students must acquaint themselves with the various chronological systems obtaining in their period. Modern dating by the *year of our Lord* was only fixed in the sixth century; and first used in this country by the Venerable Bede in the eighth. His example was followed by the imperial (German) chancery a century later, and—ironically—by the Papal chancery only in the tenth century. The historical year, which in the Middle Ages normally began on 25 March, now begins on 1 January, a date laid down in 1582 by Pope Gregory XIII when he reformed the calendar by cutting out ten days from that year. This change was adopted in Scotland in 1599, and in England and Ireland in 1751. All this makes the chronology of modern documents very complicated. Fortunately there are numerous chronological guides of which the most readily available is C. R. Cheney's *Handbook of Dates* (Royal Historical Society).

Here will also be found tables showing the date of Easter in any year, the regnal years of each king, calculated from the day of his accession to the throne, and a full list of those saints' days and festivals by which the Church preferred to date events. The medieval calendars upon which these are based vary widely from country to country, and from province to province. Confusion also arises, as Professor Cheney explains, in regard to saints who bear the same name (e.g. St Thomas the Apostle, and St Thomas of Canterbury). And there are other pitfalls, as when a feast is cited by the *Introit* read on that day. The editor of the Great Register of Lichfield Cathedral quotes a letter of 1183 from the archbishop of Canterbury bidding the proctors of the dean and chapter 'present themselves to him at [the sign] of the Man of Galilee (*ad viri Galilee*) in Caen'. He has however mistaken the place for the time, and the reference is not to an inn, but to the *Introit* for Ascension Day (Acts 1. 11: Ye men of Galilee, why stand ye gazing up into Heaven?).

GEOGRAPHY

Geography, although today a separate subject, has always been a vital aspect of history. The first thing we need to study is a map, and the most insoluble of all unanswered questions is: How far is the history of a country determined by its geography? Maps speak for themselves. As Maitland remarked 'two little fragments of the original one-inch ordnance map are more eloquent than would be many paragraphs of written discourse'. In his *Domesday Book and Beyond* Maitland used the O.S. map to demonstrate two main types of primitive settlement in Britain, the nucleated villages and the dispersed hamlets, but in fact the same map is a commentary on both earlier and later history. To assess the purely geographical factors in history is the object of 'historical geography', the study of which has been much stimulated by the rapid growth of geography as an independent subject in the last generation. Historical geographies today are the work of geographers turning to history rather than as formerly of historians learning geography. A good medieval example of this trend is H. C. Darby's *Domesday Geography of England*, which shows by maps not merely the local divisions of each county but in addition plots the distribution and density of population, woodland, pasture, fisheries, mills and saltpans as recorded in the Survey. A recent example of this frontier research is

Professor E. W. Gilbert's *University Town in England and West Germany* which is closely relevant to the urgent contemporary problem of town planning. But the geographers' first interest is the world of today, and their characteristic contribution is the steady stream of books on the new, emerging, independent states, which make admirable introductions to their subject pending deeper research into their history.

The earliest detailed maps of England, which belong to the thirteenth century, are all the wrong shape. They serve only to remind us that for nearly 1,000 years after the fall of Rome, kings ruled and armies fought with no effective assistance from maps: and another three centuries passed before the map of England attained a rough accuracy. Some indication of the way in which map-making developed during the sixteenth century may be found by comparing the maps of two harbour towns in the Public Record Office. One is of Great Yarmouth in the time of Henry VIII; the other of Whitstable and Sandwich (1584). The first, in spite of its wealth of fascinating detail, is purely pictorial. The second, a bare half-century later, is the work of a professional map-maker. It is drawn to scale, and of a quality and accuracy comparable with anything produced today.

This change is part of the general scientific development of the sixteenth century, but in England at any rate an additional impetus to accurate cartography was the rise of the professional surveyor, who was often used to map estates taken over by the new landowner classes after the dissolution of the monasteries.

Today, thanks to the Ordnance Survey (Chessington, Surrey), Britain is probably the best served country in the world with colour maps to the scale of $\frac{1}{4}$ inch, $\frac{1}{2}$ inch, 1 inch and 2½ inches to the mile, and very many more. Among these the Great Britain ten-mile series (1 : 625,000) of maps constitutes the National Atlas and is invaluable for students of land utilisation, population changes, Gas Board areas, electricity supply and so on. The Ordnance Survey has also published valuable archaeological maps of Ancient Britain to 1066: Roman Britain: Britain in the Dark Ages: and Monastic Britain. Each of these is supplied with an explanatory booklet.

The value of maps to the historian is not easily exaggerated, but they must be used properly. Our textbooks of the Middle Ages, for example, are still full of maps of campaigns and of battles (Crécy, Poitiers, etc.) which are nearly worthless, simply because there were then no accurate maps and the chroniclers' descriptions of battles were largely imaginary. Without maps there could be little strategy and not much tactics. Nor can much reliance be placed upon maps showing the boundaries settled by treaties. F. W. Maitland in his *Domesday Book and Beyond*—one of the finest examples of the 'historian at work' in our language—shows us something of the true value of maps for our earliest history. In a purely agricultural district we can safely assume that the pattern of 'a land of villages' shown in plate no. XIX is very ancient, for during the last three centuries the tendency has been against the formation of villages and towards the distribution of scattered homesteads. The purest specimens of 'a land of hamlets' are found on the Celtic fringe—Wales and Cornwall—and hamlets are also common where there were formerly great tracts of forest. See *Domesday Book and Beyond*, pages 16–17. Note that Maitland chose the earliest edition of the Ordnance Survey Map as the best for his purpose.

## ARCHAEOLOGY

Archaeology is history approached, primarily and often solely, not from written documents, but from controlled observation of surviving objects from the past. Its evidence is more unbiased, because more unconscious, than that of documents; and its scope wider than that of straight history since it ranges from prehistoric times to the nineteenth century. The discipline of archaeology, as severe as in any other branch of historical study, is bound up with its special techniques—excavation, air photography, chemical analysis, and the construction of time-scales from stratification. Contrary to the common opinion, the modern archaeologist spends more time in his study or in libraries than at the bottom of a trench! The limitations of the subject in Britain are obvious enough. For the period before the Roman occupation it has no chronology of its own. It brings to light a logical succession of cultures which have no fixed 'dates'; nor can it ever hope to give us the thoughts of individual men, although in favourable circumstances, it may tell us something of their communal life and their religion. Faced by these difficulties, archaeologists have developed uncanny skill in applying their special methods of investigation, and today no other branch of history demands so high a degree of expert knowledge and specialisation. The amateur historian, even if he does not do much good, does no harm to his materials. But the amateur archaeologist is the bane of his subject, and can easily ruin, as he has done in the past, the sites he excavates. It is thus, more than most, a subject for experts. The archaeologist carries a heavy load of responsibility, for in the last resort we have to trust the observation of individuals.

From Roman times onwards the study of archaeology is increasingly conjoined with that of written documents, and its contribution to history becomes, if not more important, at least more precise and illuminating. Yet its progress is uneven. Thanks to the survival of inscriptions and abundant comparative material in Europe, Roman archaeology is, within its self-imposed limits, an exact science. In the fifth and sixth centuries A.D., owing to the failure of written documents, and the movements of peoples, a second twilight descends upon the study of archaeology, whose exiguous achievements have been admirably summarised by Mr Noel Myres.[3] Thenceforward more progress has been made. Take, for example, Yeavering in Northumberland where an air photograph suggested and subsequent excavation has given us the complete layout of a royal palace-complex, constructed of timber. It is none other than the palace in which, the Venerable Bede tells us, Paulinus baptised and preached to the Northumbrians in the seventh century.

In the high Middle Age, with the increase of documentary sources and the more ample supply of archaeological material, the rewards are proportionately greater. Outstanding are the researches of Dr Cyril Fox, Mr Pantin[4] and others, who by dint of 'combined operations' have arranged in dated sequence the changing construction of every sort of cottage, house and homestead in which men lived across the centuries. Similar co-operative work is throwing new light on other constructions, in particular upon monastic houses and castles. The *Society of Medieval Archaeology* (London Museum, Kensington Palace, W.8) exists to further this study, whose results are summarised in an annual publication, *Medieval Archaeology*.

*The Council for British Archaeology* (10 Bolton Gardens,

London, S.W.5) issues to subscribers (5s. a year) details
of training courses and some of the sites where help is
welcomed.


## GENEALOGY AND HERALDRY

The origins of heraldry lie in the early twelfth century,
when the knighthood of western Europe began to adopt
an ordered differentiation of devices upon their shields,
whether in battle or the tournament. In a very short time
families came to be identified with and by their arms, which
had all the *éclat*—to take a modern parallel—of the racing
colours so full of meaning to all followers of the Turf.
Their arms were borne on their seals and on their tombs;
and gradually there arose the Heralds and Kings of Arms,
whose function was to administer the code of knightly
manners known as chivalry. The Heralds' College (in
Queen Victoria Street in the City) was incorporated in
1484 and refounded in 1555 by a new charter which is still
in force. By the reign of Henry VIII the old baronage was
much reduced, and Tudor policy encouraged a new race of
lords and gentry, drawn partly from knightly houses and
partly from burgess and yeoman stock. Henceforth the
main business of the Heralds' College was the verification
of the pedigrees of those whose social position indicated an
actual or potential stake in the country. The Visitations
carried out by the Kings of Arms in the sixteenth and
seventeenth centuries preserve a vast amount of heraldic
and genealogical information which, along with the
medieval rolls of arms and some valuable manuscript collections, are still preserved in the College. Thus today the
Heralds are the historian's close allies in the vital field
of genealogy; and despite the social revolution of the

twentieth century, still control the bearing of arms, whether by lords, knights, commoners or corporations. Indeed the publication of the *Complete Peerage* in fourteen massive volumes, the *English Genealogy* of Sir Anthony Wagner, Garter King of Arms, and the forthcoming *Dictionary of British Arms* suggest that interest in family origins was never greater than today.

Heraldry as a science was already complete by 1300 and has remained unchanged ever since. It preserves a complicated technical language which must be learnt by any student who wants to use heraldic evidence in order to identify, not only families, but individual members of families: there is, for example, a range of 'cadency' marks, which were added to coats of arms, and often to crests as well, to indicate a son's place in his family—and whether— if he were the eldest son—his father was alive at the time.

# 3

## TYPES OF MATERIAL

### LOCAL HISTORY AND LOCAL RECORDS

IT has often been said that all history is local history, and Domesday Book reminds us that the history of England includes that of every single estate or manor in the country. Nevertheless local history as a separate study is implied in our whole, age-long administrative structure. From the earliest times, England has been divided into shires, each with its sheriff, and separate court. The shires were sub-divided into territorial Hundreds (now abandoned) each with a court and its bailiff, containing a group of villages. The village normally had a squire and some freeholders, whose estates were known as manors. At the very bottom lay the unfree village community of peasants, who nevertheless cultivated their own 'strips' as well as those of the lord of the manor. This civil structure of society was somewhat blurred and confused by the separate ecclesiastical divisions—archbishoprics, dioceses, rural deaneries and parishes. Accordingly the historian when approaching our history from the regional or county angle, or anything smaller, is employed on local history, a subject in its own right with its own characteristic records, its own pitfalls, and its special techniques. Its independent status was established sixty years ago by that gigantic enterprise, the *Victoria History of the Counties of England*, still uncompleted but still in active progress. More recently a special Readership has been set up in the University of Leicester; and the Society of Genealogists (37 Harrington

Gardens, S.W.7) has large collections relating to local history. The National Council of Social Service (26 Bedford Square, W.C.1) also publish a useful half-crown pamphlet called *Introducing Local History*. This includes a list of County Record Offices with their times of opening and closing.

Within the larger framework, the core of local history is found in the study of the village and the village community—an inquiry no less important than that of the state, and one which, just because it has received less expert attention, is no less difficult. Indeed in the earlier part of our history, its social standing is still an unsolved problem, since its workings had no interest for the aristocratic society of early times. Already in the eleventh century it formed some sort of community, and the reeve, the priest and six men represented each village at the Domesday inquiry. But we know much less of the medieval village than of the particular estate or manor, with its lord, its villeins, its court and its court rolls; and there were often several manors in a single village. It is only since the sixteenth century when the parish was selected by the Tudor sovereigns as the unit of local civil administration that we can see the village community in action, with its open fields, its parish priest, its vestry and its village constable. At the beginning of the nineteenth century there were some 11,000 parishes in England, each of which, according to Sydney and Beatrice Webb, should possess, in addition to the parish registers, churchwardens' accounts from the fourteenth century, vestry minutes from at least the seventeenth or eighteenth century, and poor relief account not much later than these. But, in fact, owing to bad custody and public indifference perhaps half of them possess no records earlier than the beginning of the nineteenth century. Even so, however, there is in the aggregate, Mr Tate[5] tells us, 'a colossal quantity of priceless historical material'. The starting point of local history is the parish chest—with a history of its own—in which the records were preserved. Perhaps the greatest service of the recently formed County Record Offices has been their sustained effort to assemble, preserve and classify local records.

In recent years the study of local history has been greatly stimulated by the writings of Dr H. P. R. Finberg and Dr W. G. Hoskins whose *Local History in England* (1959) is the standard textbook on the subject.

## OFFICIAL HISTORY

In all ages kings and governments, whose prime function is to make history, have tried their hands at writing it: and such history must always be suspect. One of the earliest forms of official history in England is perhaps the royal genealogies of the Anglo-Saxon kings which are carried back sometimes to Cerdic and Cynric in the fifth century, and sometimes more ambitiously to Woden, Geat and Adam, the first man. In the eleventh century we encounter the Bayeux tapestry, which seems to tell us the official story of the Norman Conquest; and two centuries later in the reign of Edward I a certain Ellis Joneston had charge of the diplomatic papers relating to Gascony, from which he prepared for his government summaries of Anglo-French negotiations since the Treaty of Paris in 1259. In the same reign the overlordship of England over Scotland was 'proved' by extracts from materials supplied by the monasteries. In all these cases the history, though selective and therefore slanted, was more or less honest; but in the later Middle Ages official history takes on a more sinister aspect.

The Parliament Rolls, both at the time of the deposition of Edward II (1327) and Richard II (1399), are blatantly false records, necessitated by revolution: and the same is true of much of the evidence collected at the dissolution of the monasteries (1536-9).

Slanted history of this kind is, of course, implicit in the very idea of the national state. In the seventeenth century— the 'century of revolution'—there was a great deal of it on both the royalist and parliamentary side, and later in the eighteenth over the foundation of the U.S.A., again on both sides.

In our own day the two world wars have brought about a vast extension of official history of a rather new kind, put together scientifically and claiming to be objective. It has been lavishly financed by the governments concerned and covers both the diplomatic origins of these wars and a most detailed account of their civil and military history. Its bulk is enormous and it is still engaging the energies of many capable historians. Yet it can hardly lay claim to finality; and the task of the future historians of these wars will be to reduce this vast output to manageable proportions, using the 'war histories' as a vast quarry from which to draw their materials, and writing with the greater freedom which only time can bring.

## PLACE-NAMES

The study of place-names like that of archaeology, with which it is closely associated, is full of pitfalls for the amateur, and is best left to professional philologists. In the last thirty years the English Place-Name Society has been engaged upon a systematic survey, county by county, which has now covered nearly half the country. Already

its publications have thrown new light upon the age of the
Saxon and Norse settlements; and rather later upon the
French and feudal elements which added so many new
names. The starting point for place-name study is its
admirable *Introduction to the Survey of English Place-names*
(ed. by A. Mawer and F. M. Stenton, 1924). This was
followed in 1956 by a survey of the results of the preceding
thirty years in *English Place-name Elements* by A. H. Smith.
Two more general works have lately been published, viz.
*The Origin of English Place-names* by P. H. Reaney (1960)
and *English Place-names* by Kenneth Cameron (1961).

## ARCHITECTURE AND BUILDING

The line between archaeology and architecture, however
difficult to draw in practice, is clear enough in principle.
The one looks only to the past: the other is primarily concerned with the present and future. Like handwriting
architecture belongs to the fine arts; and it is curious that
the progress of both was greatest in the otherwise back-
ward-looking period of the Middle Ages. Medieval
churchmen were fanatical builders, ruthlessly pulling down
the work of their predecessors in their efforts to be up to
date. Only when the creative impulse began to fail in the
fifteenth century was there any return to classical models.
Nor did the Renaissance halt the itch for building, which
rather gathered force, at least in secular architecture, until
the nineteenth century. Then there arose a movement—very
powerful today—to preserve our 'architectural heritage';
and early in the present century Royal Commissions were
appointed for England, Scotland and Wales to publish
inventories of the 'ancient and historical monuments and
constructions' from the earliest times to 1707[6], and to specify

those which seemed most worthy of preservation. A great many of these elaborate and too-costly inventories, arranged by counties, have been published. Yet the work is still far from complete, owing largely to the growing complexity of the techniques used by their expert compilers, especially in the prehistoric sections. In these volumes the study of architecture and archaeology go hand in hand, and the scale of the undertaking can be gauged from the fact that the inventory for the City of Cambridge, lately published, runs to two large volumes printed in double column and profusely illustrated.

Inventories apart, the successive styles of Romanesque, Gothic, Perpendicular, Tudor, Jacobean and Georgian architecture have been minutely studied in the past century, and quite recently there has been a rapidly growing interest in modern domestic architecture. Georgian building in particular, which ties up closely with the social development of the eighteenth century, has attracted attention, integrating the purely architectural with the historical approach. Thus, Sir John Summerson[7] writes of Adam's London houses:

These houses of Adam's were not pleasure pavillions or settings for Vanity Fair; they were built by people with a certainty of their own importance and of the paramount justice of whichever political cause they espoused. They were not built for domestic but for public life—a life of continual entertaining in drawing-rooms and ante rooms and 'eating rooms' where conversation would not be wholly ephemeral. . . .

Our kings, too, from a very early period, were great builders, and the Ministry of Works has in preparation a *History of the King's Works* under the editorship of Mr Howard Colvin, extending, in five volumes, from the earliest times to the year 1852. A vast field of inquiry remains to be exploited by historians in respect of ordinary, utilitarian building as a craft—its masons, its materials and its accounts. Here the pioneer work is Mr L. F. Salzman's monumental *Building in England* (1952).

## SEALS

Seals are of great interest in themselves to the archaeologist, the antiquarian and most of all to the historian of art. Their study is also inseparably bound up with that of the documents which they authenticated. Both the formulas and structure of our charters and writs, and the very development of the administration, can only be understood in close association with the royal seals, which slowly multiplied as government grew more and more complex. For four centuries before the Norman Conquest the royal charters, of which a very large number survive, were grandiose long-winded documents which, in startling contrast to those of the German emperors and French kings, bore no seals, and seem to have been the work of ecclesiastics rather than of an organised chancery. But by the eleventh century we encounter a new development—the terse, vernacular letter, sealed with a coin, or two-faced seal of wax, by which the royal orders were conveyed to the shire courts. This little writ, taken over by the Norman kings, and translated into Latin, became the ancestor of the elaborate charters, letters patent, letters close and writs issued by the Crown until the present day. The royal writing office was in charge of the Chancellor, 'the secretary of state for all departments', who, with his staff of clerks—for there was as yet no fixed capital or centre of government —perpetually itinerated from place to place with the king, his master. In this way both the royal bounty and the royal commands were associated in the minds of his subjects, mostly illiterate, with the Great Seal. In the thirteenth century the needs of state gave rise to a new seal, the Privy Seal, which became a second, independent secretariat. A further duplication occurred in the fourteenth century with the invention of the Secret Seal or Signet kept by a new officer, the King's Secretary, and from the fifteenth to the latter part of the eighteenth century government administration was largely carried out by two Secretaries of State. In the last two centuries the transition to modern cabinet government has been achieved by increasing the number of Secretaries of State, each of which today is a Cabinet Minister. The Signet Office was, alas, abolished in the nineteenth century, as was the Privy Seal, though the Lord Privy Seal survives as a minister of the Crown: but the Great Seal is still used for patents of nobility and other important documents. No aspect of our historical development better illustrates the continuity and conservatism which characterises the slow transformation of a small feudal state into the world power of the nineteenth century.

Thus in English history, unlike that of France, the multiplication of seals involved the multiplication of secretariats. In the twelfth century the appearance of an Exchequer seal marks the growing departmental independence of the Treasury, and somewhat later the courts of law developed their special seals and secretariats. From the twelfth century onwards every great lord or bishop had his seal and his chancellor, and by a curious and unique development, in England, the practice of the great was quickly extended to the lower ranks of society. Huge numbers of land transfers sealed by the parties survive, though from the sixteenth century onwards signatures tend more and more to replace

D

seals as a means of authentication. In this late period too
there is a great increase in the use of indentures (plate X)
where the transaction required two or more identical
copies of the document.

The study of seals underlines the warning, which applies
to all administrative history, that we must not ante-date the
passing either of medieval forms of government or ways of
thinking. In both Church and State the medieval 'set-up',
however weakened, was basically intact until the third
quarter of the eighteenth century, only to be reshaped in a
revolutionary way in the century that followed. Some
other points are important to the historian:

1. The development of seals sketched above was
broadly contemporaneous in all European countries, a clear
proof that it was brought about by sheer administrative
necessity. At all stages, too, it was influenced by the Papal
Chancery, the oldest in Europe, and the most expert. The
Popes couched all their formal announcements in the form
of letters, and from the seventh century or earlier used a
coin seal of lead, pendant from the document. This no
doubt was the original exemplar of the little sealed writ, a
pioneer document which had profound effects upon other
secular chanceries.

2. The detection of forgery, so widespread in the Middle
Ages, is bound up as much with forged seals as forged
documents.

3. Seals and documents, which came in time to have
binding legal force, were in origin no more than *post-
factum* records of transactions carried out orally in courts
and before witnesses, whose testimony was thus rendered
more durable. In Anglo-Saxon times such records were
significantly described as Bookland or land for which there
was a charter. Until a comparatively late date the essential

of all land transactions lay in 'livery of seisin' or possession given by some person, either with a symbolic knife or a sod of earth or by being laid upon the altar in church.

4. In periods of general illiteracy seals, though the chief, were not the only devices used to produce authentic documents. From the tenth century onwards England made increasing use of cirographs or indentures, and there were also public notaries and scriveners. Many charters, too, were authenticated by the sign of the cross, sometimes added by the witness, but more often by the scribe. The most solemn papal grants, called Privileges, bore the autograph signatures of the cardinals. From the sixteenth century onwards the autograph signature by degrees ousted other forms of authentication.

## COINS

The study of coinage, once an antiquarian hobby, has made immense strides in the present century. This progress is the result of specialisation and new techniques for analysing its metallic composition. For example, the standard work on *Anglo-Saxon Coins*, edited by R. H. M. Dolley (1961), includes contributions from more than a dozen experts. Today no ancillary science is more important to the historian; yet none is more technical or more difficult. For early periods, when the documentary evidence is slight or non-existent, the numismatist is dependent on the chance discoveries of coin hoards, by which it is possible to trace the direction of major trading activities, to fix the boundaries of early kingdoms, to record the names of otherwise unknown rulers, and even to establish the fact that there was a coinage, as in the case of the Welsh Howel Dda in the tenth century. Somewhat later the coinage used

by barons and ecclesiastics reflects the weakness of the
central government, while later still the progress of infla-
tion is marked by the increasing depreciation of the coinage. In modern times the importance of the coinage is no
less; but with the increase of documentary evidence, the
inferences to be drawn become increasingly intricate and
require a clear grasp of economics and world trade.

NEWSPAPERS, MAGAZINES AND PAMPHLETS

The early development of newspapers and pamphlets
coincides with the abolition of the Court of Star Chamber
(1642) and the beginning of the Civil War. Between 1640
and 1660, the bookseller George Thomason, despite the
renewed repression under the Commonwealth, collected
15,000 contemporary pamphlets and over 7,000 issues of
newspapers. The Restoration was followed by the Licen-
sing Act (1662) which finally expired in 1695. The first
daily *The Daily Courant* was established in 1702; but it was
only gradually that the newspapers ousted pamphlets and
magazines as the chief vehicles of political controversy. In
the early nineteenth century the introduction of the steam
press more than quadrupled the output of *The Times*, and
by 1834 Lord Lyndhurst could describe Thomas Barnes, its
editor, as 'the most powerful man in the country'.

The study of the newspaper, the 'fourth estate' as an
organ of opinion, is thus essential for the historian of
politics, as well as for economic, social and local history.
Its value lies in the fact that it is strictly contemporary. It
is not distorted by hindsight. 'Comment is free but the facts
are sacred' were no doubt the words of an idealist, but
despite bias and propaganda, the newspaper gives a mass of
factual information unobtainable elsewhere. Until this

century newspapers were written mainly for men; and after politics their main interests were in trade, the law courts and sport. But in their advertisements (as yet hardly studied except by historians of literature and the theatre) they range beyond these masculine preoccupations.

## WILLS

Wills, which today are valued as much for their probate inventories as for the actual testaments, are among the historian's oldest documentary sources. Prior to 1857 they were a matter for the ecclesiastical courts. The wills of the wealthier people and of those who had property in more than one diocese were normally proved in the Prerogative Court of Canterbury: the remainder in the courts of the relevant bishops and archdeacons. After 1857 the wills of the Prerogative Court of Canterbury were made available in Somerset House, and the rest transferred to District Probate Registries, whence they have lately passed to County Record Offices or (in some cases) to public libraries. B. G. Bouwen's *Wills and their Whereabouts* is now being republished, edited by Anthony J. Camp.

## PAINTING AND PORTRAITURE

Pictures are visual documents. The cinema and television have immensely stimulated this approach: more and more our history books rely upon illustrations as this pamphlet testifies. The new movement is all to the good, for it makes the past more living and colourful, but it also complicates the historian's problem and makes his task more difficult. Pictures will stimulate the dullest imagination, but they can easily mislead us unless we take the trouble to master the discipline and the conventions of each medium. Take for example painting, or more precisely portraiture; by which the historian seeks to read the characters of eminent men and women in the past. There is the obvious danger of reading into the face the character indicated by the facts of their lives already known to us. Moreover, any interpretation of a portrait, as Mr Piper[8] reminds us, is subjective, and not a statement of historical fact. To make even the most modest deductions we must first acquaint ourselves with the differing fashions by which portraiture is controlled from age to age. In the Middle Ages the portrait is rarely life-like, and even from the Renaissance period since when it is infused by 'a warmer humanity', it must not be read as a literal transcription. Jacobean portraits tend to be sad; in the eighteenth century 'noses were worn lofty and long, and by the nineteenth century everyone was be-whiskered'. Nor is it safe to argue from accessories, such as hands, which, we are informed, a great painter like Reynolds usually drew from those of his servants! Portraits were, after all, works of art made to please patrons: they go hand in hand with biography, and we need to be familiar with the accepted conventions of both. Sculpture too has its own changing conventions—and so have illuminated manuscripts and monumental brasses. Illustrations, therefore, however rewarding require their own letter-press and even so have meaning only to the initiated. Our eyes can illuminate our understanding but can never be a substitute for mental effort. They actually add to our burdens. Pictures of castles, cannon[9] or armour require a study of the art of war; cathedrals and churches an architectural training: monumental brasses and coins a knowledge of the limited techniques of the engraver. And the nearer we approach to the fine arts, such as writing, sculpture and painting, the greater the need for a controlled, imaginative grasp of their respective disciplines.

## MONUMENTAL BRASSES, EFFIGIES AND MISERICORDS

All these can be pleasantly and profitably studied in parish churches and cathedrals. The earliest and finest brasses date from the reign of Edward I (1272–1307). Thenceforward the number of surviving examples increases rapidly: though there is a sharp decline in their artistic quality and workmanship in the sixteenth century. Brasses are however still numerous in the first half of the seventeenth century, after which they tail off rapidly until in the eighteenth century the art dies out altogether. For the study of women's costume, armour, the dress of priests and laymen (e.g. wool merchants) brasses are invaluable. The rubbing of brasses is a useful hobby, which is still growing in popularity; the Setvans brass here reproduced (Plate I) is taken from a rubbing made by the writer more than forty years ago. See H. W. Macklin, *The Brasses of England*, Allen and Unwin, seventh ed. 1953, or J. Mann, *Monumental Brasses*, Penguin Books, 1957. For misericords see M. D. Anderson, *Misericords*, Penguin Books, 1953. For later costume see J. Laver, *Fashions and Fashion Plates, 1800–1900*, Penguin Books, 1943.

# 4

## SOURCES OF INFORMATION

### LIBRARIES AND RECORD OFFICES

SECOND only to palaeography as a tool in the hands of the historian is some familiarity with libraries and archive depositories, where he may expect to find material relevant to his subject. It is customary to draw a clear line between the primary sources, whether printed or still in manuscript, and the secondary books, the evidence of which should be carefully studied before plunging into the original material. This may be a counsel of perfection—though this is doubtful—but in the writer's experience it never in fact works out like that. If any line is to be drawn, it should, I think, be between the original sources still unprinted and the remaining material. In practice it is not a bad plan to begin with a preliminary dip into the manuscripts, and later to pursue the subject indifferently among all kinds of evidence as the argument of the projected inquiry takes shape in one's mind.

Despite the heroic efforts of bibliographers, the problem of tracking down the relevant material is theoretically insoluble. In 1956 the British Records Association published particulars of more than 150 record depositories in Great Britain; and this list did not claim to be exhaustive, especially in regard to libraries. To this formidable list has to be added the large collections of books and manuscripts still in private hands, the proper approach to which is through the publications of the *Historical Manuscripts Commission*. This chaotic situation has a history behind it. In 1838 the records of the government, hitherto preserved in widely dispersed departmental offices, were brought together in the Public Record Office in Chancery Lane. Nothing was done about local records, which, despite the findings of the Royal Commission (1919), have never been organised in the systematic way followed, for example, in Holland, France and Belgium. Today there is normally in each county a record office run by the county council, and a record office in each borough. Separate from both are the ecclesiastical records, divided between diocesan offices and those of the dean and chapter of each cathedral. In a few exceptional instances, the records of these various authorities, or some of them, are combined in a single repository. In Scotland the government records are concentrated in the Register House, and much other material in the National Library, both in Edinburgh. Wales has its National Library at Aberystwyth and Northern Ireland its own Public Record Office at Belfast. In addition we have the extensive collections of manuscripts in the University Libraries of Oxford and Cambridge and their college libraries, and in the John Rylands Library in Manchester and similar private libraries.

Among all these repositories two are of outstanding importance, viz. the Public Record Office and the British Museum. One or the other, or both, are the normal starting point of most serious historical inquiry, and, together with the Institute of Historical Research in the Senate House of London University, they form the focal point of contemporary historical research. Admission is by ticket obtained by application to the Secretary, and being both government institutions they are at first sight forbidding by reason of their repellent architecture, their uniformed attendants and the ubiquitous policemen at the gates. But once inside the rawest student is soon put at ease by the unfailing courtesy and kindness of their expert staff whom no ignorance can surprise.

## THE PUBLIC RECORD OFFICE

The most obvious feature of the public records is their size. As separate documents they run to millions, and in bulk they weigh hundreds of tons. No other archives save those of the Vatican go so far back or are so complete. Accordingly, there never has been or could be any idea of printing them in full, though great efforts have been made to publish summary calendars of the more important classes of documents. Nor must we forget that, despite a policy of organised destruction of the more ephemeral records, their bulk increases annually at an ever-growing pace. For the convenience of searchers there is a printed *Guide* in two volumes which lists the main classes, further particulars of which are contained in hundreds of manuscript volumes in the Office. The existing *Guide* was edited by M. S. Giuseppi in two volumes, and a revised edition has now been issued.

Despite many losses and the muddles of archivists in the past, the records form an organic structure, systematically recording the growth of the State, from the simple times when all government was a function of the king's household to the multifarious departments charged with contemporary administration. The earliest public record in custody is Domesday Book, compiled before the death of William the Conqueror in 1087, and thenceforth preserved in the Treasury until the nineteenth century when it passed to the new Record Office in Chancery Lane. From the twelfth century are preserved the Pipe Rolls of the Exchequer and a few legal records; but the real starting point of the national archives is the first year of King John (1199) when the government of the day began the practice, never since abandoned, of preserving enrolled copies of all out-letters issued by the King's Chancellor and sealed with the king's seal. The Chancery Rolls in their thousands have been briefly calendared in the course of the last seventy years under the three main headings of Charters, Letters Patent and Letters Close, and so given the writing of our history a fullness of detail precisely dated never before possible. Something has also been done to make available in print a fraction of the financial records of the Exchequer, but the vast collections of the Plea Rolls and other legal records are still virtually untouched. In the post Reformation period a great part of the State Papers has been calendared, but in general the nearer we approach the present day, the more we are dependent upon the original documents. A useful handlist of public records published by the government is issued by the Stationery Office (H.M.S.O. Sectional List No. 24) and this also includes particulars of the *Chronicles* and *Memorials* published by the Master of the Rolls—the famous *Rolls Series*. Nearly a hundred major works were printed in this series, many of them, since medieval writers tend to be long-winded, running to several volumes. They include much of the best work of bishop Stubbs, who was later to write *The Constitutional History of England* to 1485; and there are other well-edited volumes, including one by F. W. Maitland. There were also, however, a large number of poorly executed volumes, and the series was halted in 1895. Part of the gap thus left is now being filled by Nelson's *Medieval Texts*, in which, unlike the *Rolls Series*, each Latin text is accompanied by an English translation.

We have already seen that the evidence of official records can no more be taken at its face value than that of the literary sources of history. As sources, the one class of evidence is no more 'original' than the other, and unless it is carefully handled record evidence is even more likely to mislead us than that of the historians and chroniclers, if only because it has the *cachet* of officialdom behind it. What then are the chief points to keep in mind when studying the Public Records?

1. They demand a clear grasp of the working of the administrative machinery, which was constantly being rearranged and adapted to changing circumstances. A single inquiry can often be pursued by the expert through the records of the Chancery, the Exchequer and the courts of law whose several operations were closely interrelated.

2. From start to finish they are full of 'common form'. In every writ the King is represented as sending his greeting (*salutem*)—not health—to the recipient, and all men of substance are commonly addressed as 'trusty and well beloved'. 'Common form' is equally evident in Diplomatic correspondence, in all transactions involving the use of a jury, and in the fictions which lie behind the 'levying' of Fines, and the 'suffering' of Recoveries, etc.

3. As in all bureaucracies, 'Parkinson's Law' was always in operation, and sheer inertia together with the vested interests of the clerks responsible led to the continuation of whole classes of documents—like the Pipe Rolls—for centuries after they had ceased to fulfil any important purpose. The historian has to distinguish carefully between 'live' classes of records and those which have become purely formal.

4. Figures and accounts are always suspect. As an ex-

ample may be cited the fifteenth-century Aulnage accounts whose deficiencies have been noted by Professor Carus-Wilson.[10] These elaborate records of taxes paid on cloth produced for sale are at first sight invaluable for the extent, locality, and organisation of England's leading industry at that time. Yet careful examination proves that names, places and amounts are alike untrustworthy, and Miss Carus-Wilson concludes that 'for the unwary the aulnager has woven an intricate web, well-nigh impossible to disentangle, ingeniously cooking his accounts, devising new patterns from old materials, and leaving behind him works of art rather than transcripts of fact!' Another example of the dangers of taking public documents at their face value is illustrated in Plate IX.

5. The public records are more valuable for what happened than for the policy and motives of men who directed events: and this limitation is more marked the more nearly we approach the present day. This is partly due to the widespread interest in history which has marked the last half-century or more. The public archives, though they are normally not open to public inspection for fifty years after the events they deal with, have been used by most governments as *pièces justificatives* for propagandist official publications relating to the two major wars of this century. The result has been to render the leading diplomatists and politicians in all countries somewhat self-conscious regarding their written orders and communications, and not much of their inner discussions and divisions which normally precede great decisions finds its way into the state papers. Private correspondence, the telephone and personal meetings at high level tend more and more to replace the leisurely progress of negotiations in an earlier age, and it is often found that a responsible newspaper correspondent is

a truer guide to the day-to-day course of events than the formal publications of governments.

6. A working knowledge of the Common Law is essential for the historian. Yet the lawyer and the historian look on the past in totally different ways; and legal historians like F. W. Maitland, who combined both disciplines, are few and far between. Much of English history consists in the struggles between the 'fictions' of the law—which are one sort of facts—and the facts of history. For example, the rule of the House of Lords that a special writ of summons to the Model Parliament of 1295 created an hereditary peerage is good law, but bad history; and the same incompatibility between law and history underlies the revolutionary events of the seventeenth century.

## THE BRITISH MUSEUM

Two of the many departments of the British Museum—all useful to the historian—are of pre-eminent importance, viz. the Department of Printed Books (King's Library, Reading Room, North Library, State Paper Room, Music Room, Map Room) and the Department of Manuscripts (Granville Library, Manuscript Saloon, Magna Carta Room, Bible Room). In the former he has access to an unrivalled library of scholarly works, elsewhere often unobtainable. The latter is a splendid, though entirely miscellaneous, collection of manuscripts including the library of the seventeenth-century antiquary, Sir John Cotton, the Harleian and Sloane collections, the Royal Manuscripts (splendidly catalogued) and the Additional Manuscripts and Charters which are constantly augmented by selective purchase. All these, barring the more recent acquisitions, are to some extent catalogued, and there is an invaluable subject index in manuscript. It is probably the largest and certainly the most important single collection in the country.

## THE HISTORICAL MANUSCRIPTS COMMISSION

### (Quality House, Quality Court, Chancery Lane, W.C.2)

The 'stately homes of England', untouched by the disastrous revolutions of continental Europe, contain many priceless, if miscellaneous, collections of family archives, still only half explored. To deal with these the H.M.C. was set up in 1859, and from 1870 to 1884 published a series of summary reports prepared by itinerant inspectors. Since that date more detailed Calendars have been published of outstanding collections, and this work still continues. In 1959 the Commission was reconstituted with wider terms of reference, including the special care of manorial and tithe documents. The Commission is an invaluable source of information regarding the discovery of documents in private hands and of access to them.

A booklet on the publications of the Royal Commission on Historical Manuscripts is published as H.M.S.O. Sectional List No. 17.

## THE NATIONAL REGISTER OF ARCHIVES

### (Quality House, Quality Court, Chancery Lane, W.C.2)

The National Register was set up in 1945 as part of the Historical Manuscripts Commission. Its aim is to record the location, content and availability of all collections of documents, other than those of the central government, in England and Wales. They include family papers, and the archives of local authorities, religious bodies, charitable organisations, business firms, schools, societies, etc.

Lists of these collections, made locally, are reproduced at Quality House, and copies distributed locally to the four copyright libraries in England and Wales, the John Rylands Library, and the Institute of Historical Research, as well as to the local record offices or libraries concerned.

Copies of all the lists (now numbering many thousands) are filed at the Register's central office, where indexes show (a) the owners and location of the documents, and (b) their contents under persons (selective), subjects, and places.

In this way a central directory to unpublished historical material is being built up, and is widely used by students and others of all nationalities. Its publications comprise the *Bulletin* issued periodically from the Register's central office, and *List of Accessions to Repositories* published annually by the Stationery Office.

PART II

# Historical Research and the
# Preservation of the Past

E

J. B. BURY in a famous lecture defined History as herself simply a science, no less and no more. He also insisted, in conflict, as I think, with his own definition, that the study of history had great practical importance for 'stripping the bandages of error from the eyes of men, for shaping public opinion, and for advancing the cause of intellectual and political liberty'. 'It is of vital importance', he remarked, 'for citizens to have a true knowledge of the past and to see it in a dry light, in order that their influence on the present and future may be exerted in right directions.'

In what directions? Recent experiments abroad have shown, indeed, that the study of history can be given a practical bias, but only at the cost of making it frankly propagandist. 'The interminable procession of history', to use Bury's own fine phrase, points no morals, though we may draw them. You cannot, in fact, make history pay a dividend. The point was put by Thomas Hobbes, who just three centuries ago found in the faculties of reason and curiosity the distinctive qualities of man; 'which makes me', he remarks, 'when I hear a man upon the discovery of any new and ingenious knowledge or invention ask gravely, that is to say scornfully, what 'tis good for, meaning what money it will bring in, to esteem that man not sufficiently removed from brutality'. The history which is a satisfaction of natural curiosity about the past is a personal thing, and it is often forgotten that there can be no teaching of history where there is no curiosity. For these the history that reads like a novel, and has about the same value, will suffice. Where there is a vital curiosity, it is not easily satisfied or put off. To such the effort to understand the past is an arduous and prolonged study, for which a whole lifetime may prove too short. Yet no other study offers the same possibilities to the average intelligence, if only it is in earnest, for none is less technical; in none is mere cleverness at a greater discount, and humility and devotion at a higher premium.

If this is indeed the true approach to history, the questions that are so persistently trailed before us appear as mere red herrings. The idea of history, for example, as 'a preparation for life' can be dismissed at once, without failing to recognise that that is precisely what, in fact, it becomes for the majority of the young men and women who study it. Or we can, with Bury, indignantly deny that history is a branch of literature, even while we are legitimately envious of our brother historians whose works run into several editions. We can, equally, oppose any conception which would assign to the more distant past any less value as history than the events of the nineteenth century, and at the same time without illogicality advise the bulk of our students to specialise on the later period. These well-worn issues are, in short, irrelevant to the nature of history as such, though they are precisely the problems with which daily life is most concerned.

The chief task of the historical teacher, apart from a general guidance, is to stimulate this natural curiosity in his pupils. And here he is faced by great practical difficulties imposed by the examination system, which casts its shadow over the whole undergraduate study of history. History, its critics are wont to object, burdens the memory without improving the understanding, and the present examination system, however unwilling our universities are to admit it, lends more than plausibility to the charge. The real problem before the teacher of history is not what to teach or how to teach it, but how to compromise with the common foe of teacher and pupil—the examination system, which converts history for many earnest students into other men's thoughts learned by heart. In this connexion it is perhaps worth reflecting that the examination system in our British universities has remained almost stationary for fifty years, though historical teaching, especially in schools, and indeed the whole conception of history, have been revolutionised in the same period. The publication of elaborate monographs in almost every part of the field has enormously increased the burden upon examinees; and those who regard this venerable system as sacrosanct may be reminded of a letter written by Professor Gregory to Lord Townshend in 1728. 'Your lordship', he wrote, 'cannot but be sensible that the methods of education in our universities have been in some measure defective, since we are obliged to adhere so much to the rules laid down by our forefathers.' Certain it is that if the flame of curiosity is to survive the repeated examinations with which, no doubt inevitably, we seek to quench it, it is only possible if historical study from the very beginning is conceived to be a sort of research.

The study of history is a personal activity—it is an individual reading the sources of history for himself. History is, or ought to be, the least authoritarian of the sciences (if that is the right word). Its essential value lies in the shock and excitement aroused by the impact of the very ways and thought of the past upon the mind, and it is for this reason that actual original documents—themselves a physical survival of that past—exercise such fascination upon those who have caught something of its secret. The late canon Foster, writing of the marvellous riches of the archives of Lincoln Cathedral, has perfectly expressed the nature of this emotion. Acknowledging the debt of inspiration he owed to a brother historian, to whom he had written about them, he says: 'Soon afterwards he paid me a visit in Lincolnshire, and it will be long before I shall forget his wonder and delight as I opened before his eyes box after box of the original charters. Each moment I expected to hear from his lips the famous "Pro-di-gi-ous" of the enthusiastic and simple-minded Dominie.' The lectures and the textbooks are a necessary preliminary, a grammar of the subject; but the purpose of all this grammar is to lead the student himself to the sources, from the study of which whatever power our writing and talking has is derived. Where this object is not achieved, we have failed. In my youth it was still common for reviewers to state that $A$ or $B$ had said 'the last word' on the difficult question of $X$, $Y$ or $Z$. The same fantastic conception still led historians to regard the sources as some dirty coal-mine, from which a precious deposit was recovered, leaving behind a vast, useless slag-heap. I would not be misunderstood: bibliography and historiography are, in their place, of the utmost importance; but the most brilliant reconstructions of the past can never lessen the immediate value of the sources for individual study.

The conception of research as synonymous with the very study of history is not really pedantic: but in fact that much-abused word has long since been identified in our common thinking with a system of higher degrees granted for theses embodying an 'original contribution to knowledge'. With one or two honourable exceptions, a deep line is drawn in British universities between undergraduate and post-graduate students. The writing of these theses is normally confined to the post-graduate students, who usually attempt one of the higher degrees, either the B.Litt. or the Ph.D. The system is largely borrowed from America (where, however, it is far more highly organised), which in turn took it from Germany. The practice of granting higher degrees has much to be said for it, and it has in any case come to stay. Nevertheless I cannot think it altogether congenial to our native outlook, and perhaps we should do well to take stock of it before it becomes quite as much an *incubus* upon English learning as it has already become in America. These 'original' theses are compiled in a very short time—one, two or at most three years: they are done by young people who have scarcely attained the equipment of a scholar by the time the thesis is completed: the choice of a subject is a perennial and notorious difficulty; and the result, at its best, is apt to be the publication of an immature monograph, much less readable than it would have been if more slowly evolved; while a very serious situation may arise for the student if, by an unlucky choice of subject, he fails to attain the degree. More generally, the student works in an atmosphere of anxiety and haste, at the very time in his career when leisure and time to think are most essential. He passes from the superficial study of wide periods (in which undergraduate work largely consists) to a specialisation that is too narrow, too intense and too hurried.

Higher degrees are bound up with the rapid development of historical teaching into a considerable profession. The demand for teachers has introduced competition which in turn threatens to commercialise historical study. It is rightly felt that the best teachers will be drawn from scholars familiar with the original sources, and the easiest proof of such familiarity is a thesis, and preferably a published thesis. Our young scholars are hard put to it to maintain the necessary quantity of 'original' research, while legitimate ambition or economic pressure urges them to hasty publication. The problem is a practical one, and to make even small changes in existing procedure would be a most complicated and difficult task. But having ventured to express my doubts about its adequacy, I will offer three general but still practical suggestions.

1. Something more should be done to efface the hard line generally drawn between under-graduate work and 'research'. Some insight into the raw material of history and the process by which the slick narrative of the text-books is evolved should be given to all honours students before they get their degrees. Experience has proved that this can be done, possibly, though not necessarily, by a thesis or exercise, which should not expect, though it might in exceptional cases obtain, publication.

2. The transcribing and editing of texts and documents should be encouraged as subjects for these degrees. At present the subjects are commonly too ambitious, and in the craze for originality the really vital and responsible work of preserving the past by publishing transcripts and calendars is commonly regarded as too humble for the grant of a higher degree. The supplicants for higher degrees would be most usefully employed in doing work for local societies, and such work, just because it is well within their compass, would lay the foundations of a surer and ultimately a wider scholarship than is achieved by the present practice. I am tempted to strengthen my case by a long list of great historians who served their apprenticeship by copying and editing texts, a list that might begin with the names of Stubbs and Maitland. But 'perhaps', wrote Maitland, 'our imaginary student is not

he that should come, not the great man for the great book. To be frank with him this is at least probable. . . . But short of the very greatest work, there is good work to be done of many sorts and kinds. . . . At least he can copy, at least he can arrange, digest, make serviceable.'

3. Post-graduate scholarships for research should be freely tenable without any obligation or pressure upon the student to enter for higher degrees. Indeed, I see no reason why theses should not be offered for these degrees, if and when they are completed, without any of the present preliminaries—in exactly the same way as those of riper years now supplicate for the D.Litt. degree. Such an arrangement would make it far easier for the examiners to insist on the proper standard, which is one of the crucial difficulties of the existing system. It would also discourage the too-hasty publication of research in book form, in favour of articles or notes in the reviews. The thesis is commonly far too long and too elaborate, the writer's single talent being hardly discoverable in the napkin of already well-ascertained truth by which it is enveloped. The contribution made by nine out of ten of these theses would go easily into a very few pages, and the verbosity which we all deplore—it must be added—is encouraged by the existing regulations.

I have sometimes wondered whether a great deal of historical research is not vitiated by our insistence upon its originality. Although we pay lip-service in our bibliographies to the just division of all historical writings into primary and secondary authorities, we are too apt to forget in practice that the true purpose of writing books about the past is not to supersede the original authorities, but to make their study more significant for our successors. What matters is that history should be studied, as

# NOTES ON THE PLATES

MOST of the plates have been chosen to illustrate points made in the text. An attempt has, however, also been made to indicate a few of the main types of material from which the historian draws his evidence, and at the same time to show that the authenticity of such evidence can never be taken for granted.

## INTRODUCTORY

*Plate I. The Setvans Brass.* 1306. Chartham Church, Kent. One of the earliest and best of English memorial brasses. The original is over six feet in length. It shows Sir Robert de Setvans. The emblem repeated on his shield and surcoat is the winnowing fan from which the family takes its name. This photograph is taken from a rubbing made by the writer.

## PALAEOGRAPHY, ADMINISTRATIVE PRACTICE AND FORGERY. PLATES II–XII

Each of these plates (with the exception of no. XI) illustrates one stage in the development of medieval handwriting. Throughout the Middle Ages handwriting was a special skill, its practice virtually confined to one small section of the population—the educated clergy. By the seventeenth century (no. VI) the handwriting of an educated layman is little different from a contemporary hand.

*Plate II. Roman Square Capitals.* Part of an inscription of A.D. 222, commemorating the provision of a water-supply for the fort at South Shields (Co. Durham). Eph. Epigr. ix, 1140.

*Plate III. Carolingian Minuscule.* About A.D. 820. The third and fourth lines are in rustic capitals, the fifth in uncials.

*Plates IV and V. Gothic Handwriting.* 1260 and 1358–63. Both examples are taken from Addit. MS 23,935 BM f. 74ᵛ and f. 574, a Dominican service book probably written in France. The first one is dated in the margin 1260. The second one shows the hand of a single quire added at the end of the book, which can be dated by internal evidence as between 1358 and 1363. It was thus written a full century later than the first, though on purely palaeographical grounds it would pass for half a century earlier. See G. R. Galbraith, *Constitution of the Dominican Order, 1216–1360.* Manchester U.P., 1925.

*Plate VI. Handwriting of James I.* Extract from the instructions for questioning Guy Fawkes. 1605.

*Plate VII. Forged Charter of William I.* Confirmation to Coventry Abbey of the gifts of its founder, Earl Leofric. The charter passed as genuine until the late Professor James Tait showed that William fitz Osbern could not have appeared in any genuine document with Peter, bishop of Chester. The seal has since been shown to be also a forgery.

*Plate VIII. Charter of William II.* Charter confirming the gift of lands by Ivo Taillebois to Peterborough Abbey (1094–8). This document, a product of the royal Chancery, is a curious mixture of the Old English (i.e. pre-Conquest) sealed writ and the continental diploma on which the grantor and witnesses made the sign of the cross. It bears the great seal of William II and the signa of the king, William Giffard, Chancellor, Roger Bigot, William Peverell and Eudo Dapifer. See T. A. M. Bishop and P. Chaplais, eds. *Facsimiles of English Royal Writs to A.D. 1100:* presented to V. H. Galbraith. Nos. xix–xx. O.U.P., 1957.

*Plate. IX. Endorsement to Writ of Summons for the Wiltshire Parliamentary Boroughs, 1433.* This shows the first few lines of a hitherto unpublished endorsement of the writ sent to the Sheriff of Wiltshire, instructing him to inscribe the names of representatives elected by the Wiltshire boroughs to the Parliament of 1433. On it the names of the boroughs (New Sarum, Wilton, Devizes, Marlborough, Malmesbury, Calne, Chippenham, etc.), in the second column the names of the burgesses, and in the third column the names of the mainpernours or sureties for the burgesses' attendance.

The names of the burgesses are normal—Long, Warwyk, Whithorn, Forster, etc.—but those in the final column begin:

'Thomas God
Johannes Save

Henricus Alle
Ricardus This
Johannes Faire . . .'

Having gone so far, the transcriber will be inclined to read the surnames in this column consecutively. If he does so, this is what he will find:

'God save alle this ffayre compayne ande gyffe theym grace weel fforto spede ffor ffayne wold they bee ryght mery thus too pray hyt hys nede (to) Gode thatte alle this worlde ganne made ande ffor usse dyed apon the rode (rood) tree save usse all.'

It is clear from this that the obligation to provide sureties for the burgesses' attendance had become a formality; and this point is confirmed by the Wiltshire endorsements to some of the earlier parliaments in the fifteenth century: clerks who wrote WILLELMUS ROBIN followed by RICARDUS HOOD, or HENRICUS LYTTEL followed by ROBERTUS JOHN are presumably making up the names they inscribe. These fictions illustrate the danger of reading medieval documents literally. Further study might prove that they were of local interest only, but if they should be typical of borough representation in the early fifteenth century, they could help to establish one of two things: that the surety was inadequate to the task of assuring the member's presence in parliament, or that his function had become unnecessary because parliamentary attendance was proving to be an asset to the boroughs as well as a disagreeable obligation to the burgess.

It is from questions like this that a small detail can proliferate into a full-scale inquiry.

*Plate X. Final Concord (A.D. 1272), Showing the Foot and the Two Indentures.* A Fine was the amicable settlement of a fictitious suit in the Court of Common Pleas by which freehold property was transferred or otherwise settled. The earliest Fines go back to the reign of Henry II. They continued until the reign of Queen Victoria, and were in great demand for securing a better title to land. The Foot of the Fine was kept by the Court, and the two indentures by the parties.

*Plate XI. Tally Stock and Foil.* Tallies were wooden receipts given by the Exchequer for sums of money paid into it. They were made of hazel wood, on which notches were cut to show the amount of the payment, and other details were written on the two sides. The stock was then slit longitudinally for the greater part of its length, and the two pieces, known as the stock and the foil, kept respectively by the sheriff or other official and the Exchequer. A detailed account of the making of tallies is contained in the twelfth-century *Dialogue Concerning the Exchequer* by Richard Fitzneale, the treasurer. They were finally abolished in 1826.

*Plate XII. Matthew Paris on his Deathbed.* Matthew Paris, the most famous of English chroniclers, became a monk of St Albans Abbey in 1217, and died in 1259. His voluminous writings have come down to us almost intact, and we are not surprised to learn that he 'constantly revolved in his heart the saying that "laziness (otiositas) is the enemy of the soul".' He was also a fine artist and freely illustrated the books he wrote. This portrait of him was the work of an anonymous continuator of his Chronicle from 1259, who remarks that what follows 'may be ascribed to another brother who, as he is unworthy to undo the latchet of his shoe has not deserved to have even his name mentioned on the page'.

AERIAL PHOTOGRAPHY. PLATES XIII–XV

Within the last twenty-five years aerial photography has added very considerably to our knowledge and understanding of the geographical and architectural shape of Britain, especially during the prehistoric and medieval periods. The Cambridge Air Surveys (General Editors, David Knowles, J. K. St Joseph and H. Godwin) have demonstrated the striking use which can be made of this technique. Aerial photography can show contours and unevennesses which it is difficult to see on the ground, thus helping to plot sites of villages or houses which have been destroyed. It can also provide evidence of the way in which the land has been settled and farmed, or trace the course of an ancient road by linking sections separated by medieval and later cultivation (no. xiv). More dramatically, an air photograph of open country on which a crop is ripening can reveal the outline of buildings which formerly existed on the site even if nothing at all is visible above the ground. This is because grain tends to ripen more quickly over hardened foundations. Plates XIII and XV both illustrate this phenomenon.

*Plate XIII. Caistor next Norwich.* This photograph of the site of the Roman camp—the first of its kind—was taken by the R.A.F. during the summer of 1928, and published in *The Times* on 4th March, 1929. The ripening barley which then covered the field thus showed not only the streets as intersecting white lines, but also the sites of the more important buildings—e.g. the twin temples visible in the centre of the picture. As a result it was possible for digging to start at once on the most interesting parts of the site.

*Plate XIV. A Section of Stane Street, the Roman Road from London to Chichester*

*Plate XV. Maiden Castle, a hill-fort or tribal* oppidum *of the late Iron Age, near Dorchester, Dorset.* Excavation has provided dramatic evidence of the assault and attack of this hill-fort by Roman troops at the time of the Roman invasion of Britain. The evidence for a small earlier enclosure embracing the eastern part of the hill-fort will be noted, also the elaborate development of the defences.

THE GREAT SEAL. PLATES XVI and XVII

*Plate XVI. The Second Great Seal of Elizabeth I. Seal.* The seal used from 1586 to 1603. The queen with orb and sceptre. A mantle, descending from her shoulders, is held off from her arms by a hand and arm issuing from clouds. On each side a shield charged with the arms of France and England quarterly, encircled with an inscribed Garter. Above each side a Tudor rose.

*Counterseal.* The queen on horseback. Note the harp. Above the queen's head the inner border is broken by an arch of clouds, from which rays issue downwards. Legend on both sides: ELIZABETHA DEI GRACIA ANGLIE FRANCIE ET HIBERNIE REGINA FIDEI DEFENSOR. The title 'Defender of the Faith' was acquired by Henry VIII before his breach with the Papacy. He also styled himself 'Lord of Ireland' not King.

*Plate XVII. The Second Great Seal of the Commonwealth. Seal.* A map of England (including Wales) and Ireland, the Channel Islands and the Isle of Man. No part of Scotland or France is shown. In the upper part of the seal is an oval shield charged with the Cross of St George. In the lower field of the seal is another oval shield bearing the Arms of Ireland. Beyond the band upon which the legend is placed is a thin border bearing a series of small oval shields charged with the Cross of St George and the Harp of Ireland alternately. Legend: THE GREAT SEALE OF ENGLAND 1651. Actual size 5¾ inches.

*Counterseal.* The House of Commons in session, with the speaker in the Chair, a member addressing the House, two clerks at the table, upon which the mace is laid. The walls of the Chamber are ornamented with spiral pilasters, with fruits and flowers between. Beyond the band upon which the legend is placed is a thin border, bearing a series of small oval shields charged with the Cross of St George and the Harp of Ireland alternately. Legend: IN THE THIRD YEARE OF FREEDOME BY GOD'S BLESSING RESTORED 1651.

## THE FINE ARTS

*Plate XVIII. The Wilton Diptych: An Unsolved Problem.* The left-hand panel shows Richard II wearing a scarlet gown embroidered with golden harts in wreaths of broom-cods. A collar of broom-cods is round his neck, and on his breast a badge of the white hart (his livery) on a black ground. Behind him stand his three patron saints: St John the Baptist with the Lamb, St Edward the Confessor with the ring he gave to the beggar, and St Edmund, King of East Anglia, holding the arrow with which he was killed by the Danes. The eleven angels in the opposite panel wear the livery of the white hart, and one of them holds upraised the banner of St George. The reverse shows a shield, surmounted by a helmet crested with a crowned lion passant guardant, standing on a cap of maintenance. The shield bears the arms of Edward the Confessor impaled with those of England. The other panel shows the livery of the white hart.

Scholars and artists alike are at odds regarding the purpose of the picture and the date when it was painted, though expert opinion is now decidedly in favour of it being an English painting by an English painter. It would seem natural to associate the picture with Richard's accession to the throne as a boy of ten and a half in 1377. But Miss M. V. Clarke showed in 1931 that the picture was not earlier than 1395 or so, about which time the King of France gave Richard II a collar of broom-cods, and the king first began to quarter the arms of Edward the Confessor with his own. It could, then, belong to the later years of the reign, but how unlikely this is will be appreciated by anyone familiar with the effigy of the king (and his first wife, Anne) in Westminster Abbey. We are thus driven to associate the Diptych with the cult which quickly arose after his murder in 1399–1400. A cult which was focused, not on his sanctity, but on the memory of his person and prerogative, and points the way towards the 'divine right of kings' of a later age. There are obvious difficulties about this, as about the many other solutions that have been advanced regarding the Diptych, and there will always be those who, trusting their eyes more than the evidence, accept the view of Mr Everard Green before Miss Clarke wrote, that it was a votive offering by Richard at his coronation to the shrine of Our Lady of Pewe.

See M. V. Clarke, *Fourteenth Century Studies*, no. viii. O.U.P., 1937; V. H. Galbraith, 'A New Life of Richard II' (in *History*, March 1942); F. Wormald, 'The Wilton Diptych' (in *Journal of the Warburg and Courtauld Institutes*, Vol. xvii, nos. 3–4); Margaret Rickert, *Painting in Britain: The Middle Ages* (Pelican History of Art) Penguin Books, 1954. Panofsky, Erwin, *Early Netherlandish Painting*, Cambridge, Mass. 1953, L. 118.

## MAPS

*Plate XIX. A Land of Villages and A Land of Hamlets. Left.* On the border between Oxfordshire and Berkshire.

*Right.* On the border between Somerset and Devon. These fragments of the Ordnance Survey map illustrate two main types of primitive settlement in Britain, the nucleated villages and the dispersed hamlets.

## WHO WROTE ASSER'S LIFE OF ALFRED?

*Plate XX. Copy of commencement of the Lost Manuscript of 'Asser's Life of Alfred'.* The manuscript was destroyed by fire in 1731. This copy, taken from Wise's edition (1722), is the only evidence we have of the handwriting of the manuscript.

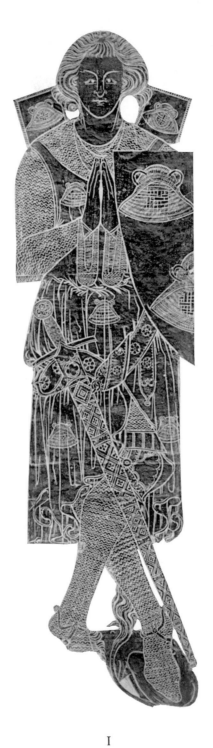

I

II

IMP CAES DIVI SEVER
NEP DIVI M ANTONINI
M AVR SEVERVS AVG PONTIFM
PIVS FELIX AVG PONTIFMS
TRIB P P COS A Q AM

III

delib; fuif comprobatæ ē exquorum numerofunt ē illi dequib; dictaur. et omnif
populuf audienf et cpublicani; iuftificauerunt dm. amē—:

EXPLICIT LIBER SECVNDVS.

INCIPIT LIBER TERTIVS.

SANCTISSIMO MARIÆ PRÆNITENTIS hISTORIA quÆ TU
nofer in lucam caput ē libri. ecfi oblaborem legentaum minuendum
numenda tur rendo rerum tamen fecundi libri nexura finem recfpicit

**IV**

Incipiunt constituciones
ordinis fratrum predicatorum.
Quoniam ex precepto regu-
le tenemur hre cor u-
num. et aiam unam
in dño: iustu est ut q
sub una regla z uni-
us pfessionis uoto uiuimus. uniformes
in obseruantiis canonice religionis in-
ueniamur: quatin unitate q interius
seruanda e in cordibz. foueat z repsen-
tet uniformitas exterius seruata i mo-
ribz. Qd pfecto eo sperituz z pleni ppt
obseruari: si ea q agenda sr scripto fue-
rint comendata: si omnibz qualit sit ui-
uendu: scriptura teste ninoteleat. Si
mutare ut addere: ut minuere: nulli
nrq ppia uolutate liceat: ne si mima
neglexerim? paulati defluam? Ad hec
tm prelatis in conuentu suo dispensan-
di cum fratribz habeat potestatem. cu sibi
aliqn uidebitur expedire: in iis papue
q studium ut predicationis ut aiaru fru-
ctum uidebuntur impedire: cum ordo nr
specialit ob predicatione z aiaru salute.
ab initio noscatur institutiis fuisse: et
studium nrm ad hoc debeat principalit
intendere: ut primo aliabz possimus
utiles esse. Priores etiam utantur di-

**V**

Modus faciendi professione talis est.
Ego. f. facio professione et promitto
obedientiam dõ et be marie z tibi dominico z
sucessoribz tuis secdm regulam bi augustini z
institucões ordis fratrum predicator q
ero obediens z tuis qz sucessoribz usq ad mortem. Cum aut sit alij prion auanq; sic
facienda est. Ego. N. facio pfessione et promitto dõ et beate marie et beato dominico
et tibi. N. prior tali loci uice. N. magri
ordinis fratrum pd. z sucessor eius secdm regulam bi augustini et institucones fratrum
ordis predicator q ero obediens tibi tuisq;
sucessoribz usq ad mortem. Nouicior aut
uestes in eorum professione bñdicantur hoc
modo. Ostende nobis domine misericordiam tua.
Et salutare tuum da nobis. Dominus nobis.z. Oremus.

Domine ihu xpe q tegumen oris.
… mortalitatis induere dig-
natus es: obsecramus imense
tue largitatis clementiam ut
hoc genus uestimentor qd sci
pres ad inocencie et humilitatis indiciu
ferre sancierunt: ita benedicere digneris
ut qui hoc usus fuerit te induere mereatur.
per dominum nostrum. ostrendum a seruate

**VI**

quhair upon it shoulde seeme that he hadi bene ~~recommanded~~ raccomendit by
some personnis to his maisteris seruice only for this use, quhairin only he
hath seruid him, & thairfore he wolde ~~not~~ be asked in quhat company also
he went out of englande, & the porte he shypped at, & the lyke questions
wolde be ~~not~~ asked anent the forme of his returne, as for these trompet
wairis founde upon him, the signifacation & ~~used~~ use of euerie one of
thaime wolde be k howin, & quhat I haue obseruid in thaim, the bearar
will show you, now luke ye remember of the crewallie villanouse ~~...~~
that rayled upon me for the name of brittaine; if I remember ride
it spake some thing of haruest & prophecied my destruction about this
tyme, ye maye thinck of this for it is lyke to be the laboure of suche a
desperate fellow as this is, if he will not other wayes confesse, the gentle
torturis are to be first usit unto him, & Sic per gradus ad ima tendum;
& so god speede youre goode worke.

James R

VIII

VII

Summa victum... Georgii... com p(re)d... et p(ar)liament... d(omi)ni Regis ap(u)d...

...in com... Octab... p(u)lt(ri)... anno Regni Regis Henri... Regis post conqu... vicesimo

Eodem... Jurat... fuit Angl... anno quilterm... elect(i) de p(ar)liament... p(re)d(i)c(t)um

Eodem... fuit comp... a(n)no quilterm... elect(i) de p(ar)liament... p(re)d(i)c(t)um

Civitas London...

Eodem... ...vino...u... Civitatis p(re)d(i)c(t)... elect(i) ad p(ar)liament... p(re)d(i)c(t)um

Eodem... Civitatis... anno... Civitatis p(re)d(i)c(t) elect(i) ad p(ar)liament... p(re)d(i)c(t)um

Burgenses Wilton...

Eodem... ...anno Burgen... Burgi... elect(i) de p(ar)liament... p(re)d(i)c(t)

Eodem... anno Burgen... Burgi... elect(i) de p(ar)liament... p(re)d(i)c(t)

Burgenses...

Eodem... concurr... anno Burgen... Burgi... elect(i) ad p(ar)liament...

IX

X

XI

XII

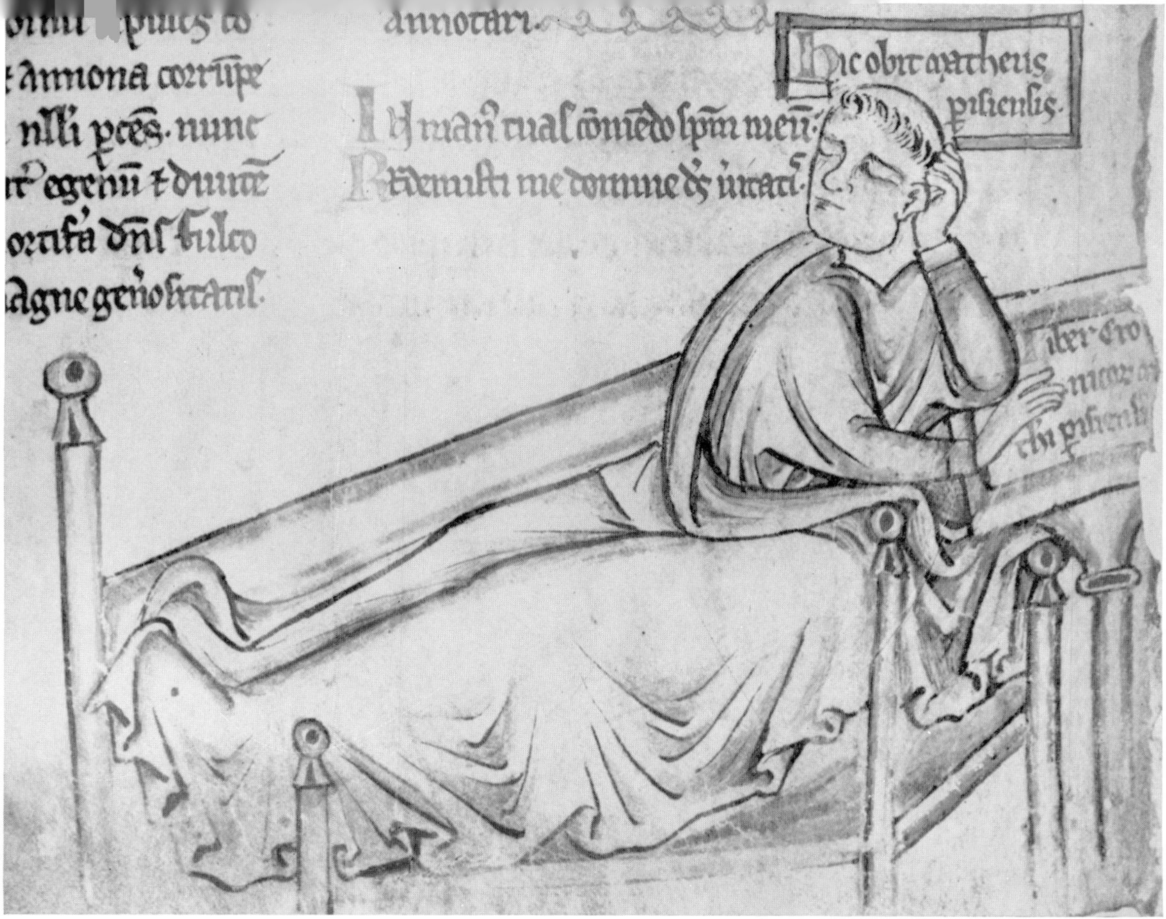

XIII

XIV

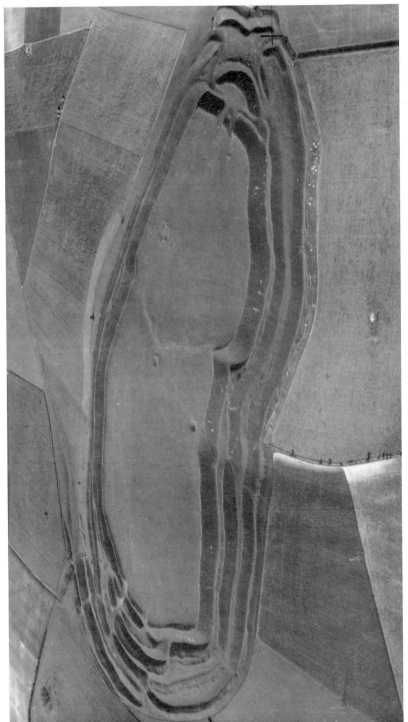

XVI

XVII

XVIII

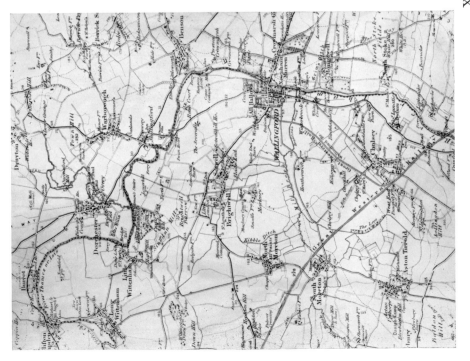

XIX

Domino meo venerabili piissimoque. omnium Brittannie insulae xpiano rum. rectori. ælfred. anglorum saxo num. regi. asser. omnium. servo rum dei ultimus. mille modam advota desideriorum. utriusque vitae. prosperitatem.

ANNO DOMINCÆ incarnationis. dccc. xlix. natus est ælfred angul saxonum rex in uilla regia que dicitur uuanating uilla paga que nominatur berrocscire que paga taliter uocatur aberrocsilua ubibuxus habundan tissime nascitur cuius genealogia taliter taliser ie

soon and as far as possible, in the original sources; the originality of the result can safely be left to take care of itself, and is in any case beyond our control. The very conception of research is borrowed from the natural sciences, and it is arguable that in learning the method of science we have too slavishly copied its methods. It is obvious that the historical material available for research is strictly limited in amount, and there is a limit to the methods of inquiry which can be employed. On those aspects of history which are most central and worthy of study, original work in the sense of discovery must surely be the exception rather than the rule. On most lines of inquiry a prolonged study of the original sources is needed merely to reach, or to try to reach, the level of our predecessors. The greater part of such work is not 'original', but it is not therefore useless. Viewed across a lifetime, it is rather the main part of one's research, the condition of those occasional publications, which are in reality its by-products. If this be true, it follows that the subjects treated by aspirants to higher degrees become, and must become increasingly, trivial and abstruse, owing to the current demand for originality. I confess myself to be in imperfect sympathy with the popular conception of an army of young and eager experts, organised and equipped for the conquest of History, methodically dividing up among themselves the country to be occupied, and never resting until the last foot of ground is conquered. One may even doubt whether significant research can be done to order at all. There is something of the accidental about all discovery, which has often only an oblique connexion with the study which led to it. The attempt to organise and direct the human mind on its highest level of activity removes the spontaneity which is its essence, and finds the motive for research in the result to be obtained instead of in the process and the activity themselves. To look back at the vast researches of our predecessors is to realise that their results, important as they were, are in some degree ephemeral, and though much stands fast for future generations, perhaps more is superseded. The activity of research, on the other hand, invaluable to those who pursue it, and to their generation, is perennial, unchanging and significant. Behind the obvious criticisms to which the system of higher degrees is, like any system, open, there is, in my mind at any rate, this deeper uneasiness.

The common assumption that the original sources would yield their last secrets to concerted research derives immediately from the school of objective historians of which Acton was the most prominent. They were sustained by an optimistic belief in the possibility of attaining, and that very shortly, to ultimate historical truth. 'Ultimate history cannot be obtained in this generation', says the *Cambridge Modern History*, 'but so far as documentary evidence is at command, conventional history can be discarded, and the point can be shown that has been reached on the road from the one to the other.' History was becoming scientific: the long conspiracy against the knowledge of truth was at an end, and competing scholars all over the world were taking advantage of the change: the splendid researches of his own generation, continued but a little further, would cause all historians of goodwill, irrespective of creed, to converge along a single line of truth. Acton was fascinated, as nearly all his generation were, by Ranke, whose critical and colourless, though not lifeless, writings appeared to that generation, within the limits he had set himself, to be the last word and a model for the future. It was in this spirit that Bury, carried away by the dangerous doctrine of development in history and the incontrovertible achievements of research, defined history as herself a science. In the last generation attention has rather turned to its practical limitations. The sure results of historical research rarely find a large audience. The big questions which lead men to write books, as well as others to read them, are still answered, and perhaps always will be answered, with conflicting voices. To be a Frenchman or an Englishman, a Protestant or a Catholic, even a poor man or a rich man, implies a limitation in outlook which is insuperable in practice, and which makes it almost inconceivable that the commonest historical questions will ever receive an agreed answer.

Thus no one today subscribes to Acton's faith in its entirety. The mildest criticism would be that it rests upon an exaggerated respect for the historical expert. The new presbyters of history are but old priest writ large, and had Acton's views been accepted at their face value, would have produced in R. H. Gretton's words, 'a kind of sacred college of historical pundits'. The threatened development never occurred. Instead we have today national groups federated by the International Historical Congress, which frankly admits the national and racial differences of interpretation of history which exist, and endeavours to mitigate them by social and learned intercourse. For the rest, the taste of historians themselves, as well as of their public, has moved towards a more subjective history: there is no longer any fear of 'the domination of one intelligence', or the individual synthesis. History is once more consciously, almost self-consciously, allying itself with literature. Clio has prevailed over Ranke, and we are no longer ashamed of the personal angle or the purple patch. In France, which does nothing by halves, the cult of the *synthèse* has gone to great lengths. British historians are moving more slowly in the same direction, and there is a certain confusion between the old ideas and the new. There is, on the one hand, a large output of 'research', which is frankly unreadable; on the other, an ever-growing number of popular syntheses which win little or no acceptance. The one type seems, at least to the outside observer, to become more and more minute in its objects, the second more and more subjective, personal and irresponsible. Our leading historical writers, aware of the difficulty, take refuge in very short periods or in biographies, on which they write readable books on old-fashioned lines. They seek the justification of a popular circulation, and are even apologetic when they themselves or others write mere learned books for the learned.

Our present difficulties, clearly traceable as far back as Acton in the nineties of the last century, find their roots in the decay of a historical philosophy which is still older. This, the Victorian view of History, depended, as everything Victorian depended, on the assumption of finality, that beyond Victorianism the force of nature could no farther go. To grasp it in its fullness we must go back to Thomas Arnold, Regius Professor of History at Oxford: better known to us—and the fact is not irrelevant—as headmaster of Rugby School and the virtual creator of the public-school system. Arnold believed his own age to be the culmination of human history. 'We have', he said, 'the full amount of earth's resources before us, and they seem inadequate to supply life for a third period of human history.' This pronouncement had immense weight with his successors, and preposterous though it be, is still not without force, if not over the minds of men, at least on their unconscious assumptions. From it all else followed. Research was mere antiquarianism: what mattered was a lively interest in the present. 'The past is reflected to us by the present; so far as we see and understand the present, so far we can see and understand the past: so far but no further.' This topsy-turvy doctrine he illustrated from the then recent *History of Greece* by Mr Mitford, who had, as Arnold naïvely put it,

described the popular party in Athens just as he would have described the Whigs in England. . . . His knowledge of the Greek language was limited, and so was his learning altogether; but because he was an English gentleman, who felt and understood the state of things around him and entered warmly into its parties, therefore he was able to write a history of Greece.

Arnold, the very type and embodiment of Victorianism, typified the Victorian idea of history, and his conceptions lie at the base of the historical curriculum of every British university today. They involved the assumption that 'man is in truth ever the same', and in due course gave rise to Freeman's famous doctrine of the Unity of History. Freeman, partial like his contemporaries to sentiment and melodrama, saw all history as a play of which his own age was the triumphant Act 5. European history, from its first glimmerings to our own day, 'is one unbroken drama, no part of which can be rightly understood without reference to the other parts which come before and after it'. This doctrine of the splendid present had the paradoxical effect of concentrating research upon the remote past, to the exclusion of contemporary or nearly contemporary history. The best-known historical books of the period rarely got past the Act of Settlement, and almost never past 1815, which for long remained the *terminus ad quem* of historical studies in university examinations.

The historical understanding of a man like Acton was of course on a much higher plane than that of the Headmaster, though he was still influenced by the Arnold tradition. A far deeper influence was the immense development of historical research in the intervening generation, under which the younger men like Bury had already passed to a wider conception of history by the close of the nineteenth century. Today the Victorian ideas are passing away before our eyes. Consider, for example, the last words of Mr H. G. Wells, no less than Arnold a child of his age, in his recent *Short History of the World*. 'Man is still only adolescent', says Mr Wells, clinging to metaphor. 'As yet we are hardly in the dawn of human greatness. What man has done forms but the prelude to the things that man has yet to do.' It may be doubted whether what is wrong with the world today is adolescence. To explain the past in terms of an ideal future would be as much a form of propaganda as to explain it in terms of the present. The old dogmatism about the present has, however, finally disappeared, and there is no longer any danger of one's contemporaries—unless it be from ignorance—describing the popular party at Athens just as though they were the Whigs. All history is contemporary history, no doubt, in the sense that it is seen through the medium of living minds. All curiosity, moreover, however apparently disinterested, springs from some present need, an individual deep-seated questioning. In this sense the present can never be eliminated from the study of the past. But at least we may claim that our curiosity is better directed today and leans—in Professor Tout's phrase—to the study of the things that were important *then* rather than to the things that are important *now*. The decay of Victorian prosperity and of the complacency which accompanied it accounts in some measure for our different outlook. The greatest period of historical writing in all French history was the generation that followed 1870, and perhaps we, too, may have gained something from our very loss of faith in our own institutions. However that may be, it is certain that we are more ready to believe today that human nature, like everything else, changes, and that history only repeats itself with a difference which, as Professor Pollard has recently remarked, generally makes all the difference. The thoughts of men are never at a stand, they change from generation to generation; and if institutions or doctrines appear to survive for centuries, it is only with an ever-changing meaning. The past is dead—dead as the men who made it. To sink oneself in even the recent past, then, is a hard discipline, but a necessary one if written history is not to be a vast anachronism.

To approach history as it were from the other end, is to learn humility at the cost of conviction and conceit. To live in any period of the past is to be so overwhelmed with the sense of difference as to confess oneself unable to conceive how the present has become what it is: it is, above all, to regard the study of the original sources not as a preliminary drudgery to the making of 'history', but as its most significant function. Such an attitude, it must be allowed, is not likely to produce a Gibbon or even a Macaulay. But if it makes the writing of history far more difficult, it informs the teaching of history with a new life and reality. The learning of history from the very beginning may become a sort of research whose primary object is an imaginative reconstruction of a different world: a personal effort to make the past, as it was, as much alive as the present. This can only be done by the study of the original sources. It is significant that Keats, who caught the nature of history in a famous sonnet, found his highest inspiration not in the Mr Mitford of his day, but in Homer.

In a conception of this kind what really matters in the long run is not so much what we write about history now, or what others have written, as the original sources themselves. They are an inexhaustible and an invaluable inheritance, to every part of which the historians of each succeeding generation will perpetually refer, if knowledge is to avoid that touch of perversion and monstrosity familiar to us from the periods when it was studied at second hand. The power of unlimited inspiration to successive generations lies in the original sources, and the work of reconstructing the past will end only with the destruction of the evidence for it. A great awakening to the value of the sources for history was indeed a mark of the nineteenth century, and a series of Royal Commissions, the latest of which reported early in the present century, effected most salutary reforms in the custody of the 'public records and of local records of a public nature'. Beyond these lies a vast category of private records, far richer than any other country can boast, which have never been subjected to any form of regulation. These private records are no less valuable for historical study than the public records themselves, and it would be the greatest mistake to imagine that even the history of the State itself and of public administration can be studied without them. Yet their very extent is unknown; they are often inaccessible; they are not always properly preserved from decay or the danger of fire, and, above all, the finest collections are continually being dispersed by sale. The Master of the Rolls, it is true, has already given a lead in the preservation of manorial Court Rolls, and a great deal is being done by the British Records Association, the Council for the Preservation of

Business Archives and the numerous local record societies. But however much is done by individuals, some form of State regulation and financial assistance is also necessary. At present our governors, though well meaning, are still museum-bound and millionaire-minded. At their best they are collectors who can be induced to buy, but only to buy exhibition pieces, whose value is a scarcity value. The purchase of old pictures, medieval psalters, original signatures, first editions, and the maintenance of derelict castles and abbeys are a sign of goodwill. But this subliterate interest in the past, excellent in itself, should be the beginning rather than the end of governmental generosity. The safety and integrity of private collections are a much more pressing need.

Not less important than the immediate physical preservation of the original sources of history is the task of putting them into print. The history of classical Greece and Rome reminds us that only that material survives which exists in many copies. More recently, we may recall the irreparable loss to Irish history by the destruction of the records in the Four Courts, or the wastage that must be going on today in Spain and in China. These are very real dangers and very near. Here again we have a right to expect that the enthusiasm and labour of historians should be helped out by more systematic and better-planned financial assistance from the government. The printing of the national archives is the task of H.M. Public Record Office. At the present rate of expenditure, so far from catching up on the past, which was the original intention in printing them, we are actually losing ground. If this continues, the progress of historical knowledge will gradually slow down. Each generation of scholars must look forward to being in a worse position than that which preceded it. The printed material, easily available for study, will become ever less and less in relation to the task to be performed by historians, and the work of synthesising the vast accumulation of material in monographs will in time become impossible. Meanwhile, as knowledge suffers, the danger of a breach in our historical tradition increases. At a modest estimate we have thirteen hundred years of continuous written records behind us. By far the greater portion of that record is still unprinted, and therefore in jeopardy. In the precarious international situation of today what is required is an effort to secure its only final preservation in print, not relatively equal to that of the Victorian age of splendid isolation, but an effort and expenditure relatively ten times greater. With each generation the tradition lengthens, and with the labours of our historical writers it also deepens. But we can only postulate for our descendants a fuller understanding of national history than we possess if we do everything in our power to preserve its past intact.

# PART III

*Research in Action*

SOONER or later, the historian, however personal and private his study, is likely to reach the point at which he wishes to summarise his conclusions in print; and no one who has attempted to 'write up' his research can fail to be aware of the wide gulf which separates merely thinking from cold print. The rules for writing a thesis or learned book are quickly found to be no more than counsels of perfection, and often raise more difficulties than they solve. It is therefore here proposed to examine some of the difficulties that surround the presentation in print of any inquiry, however small. With this end in view a particular problem is considered in detail below, preceded and followed by a commentary on the method pursued. For this purpose we require a significant question, capable—at least in theory—of a definite answer. There is at hand a copy-book example in the Latin Life of King Alfred the Great which purports to have been written by Bishop Asser, his friend and helper, who died as bishop of Sherborne in A.D. 910. The question to be decided is whether this life was written by Asser in the year 893, when the king was still alive, or by someone else in the eleventh century, to which the only known manuscript (now destroyed) belonged. It is peculiarly apt to our purpose, since virtually all the research necessary has long since been printed in W. H. Stevenson's masterly edition of the Life.[1] After careful examination Stevenson, somewhat hesitatingly, accepted the Life as genuine, though he

[1] Clarendon Press, 1904. Reprinted in 1959 with an article on recent work by Professor Whitelock. Translations by L. C. Jane (King's Classics) and E. Conybeare, *Alfred in the Chroniclers* (London, 1900).

had to admit that this conclusion left many difficulties un-explained. In particular Asser's picture of the king as all his life a sick man, almost a sick monk, was hard to reconcile either with the picture of the splendid warrior given by the Anglo-Saxon Chronicle or that of the scholar king sup-plied by the famous Prefaces to Alfred's translations. There were, too, other difficulties which have never been cleared up, and to me at least after sixty years the view that the Life was an unsuccessful eleventh-century attempt to harmonise these two has become not less but more likely than in 1904.

The form and contents of the Life are both unusual and require a brief description. Its basis is a much-embroidered translation of the Anglo-Saxon Chronicle, into which the author has inserted many new facts regarding the king and his family: e.g. his birth at Wantage in 849, his mother's name, and details of his marriage and of his children. The translation begins at the year 849 and extends to the year 886. This chronological framework is interrupted from time to time by accounts of the king's boyhood (chapter 21), of his private life and manners after his marriage (c. 73), and of his family (c. 75). These passages repeatedly affirm Alfred's love of the 'liberal arts', of Saxon poetry, and above all his piety and zeal for learning. The king, despite his prowess in war, is pictured as an invalid, who suffered all his life from diseases: first, from a disease variously described as congenital and as acquired by prayer; later, from another disease miraculously acquired by further prayer (c. 74). There are besides a number of 'good stories', such as the story of Eadburh, the daughter of Offa, trying to marry Charles the Great, the story of Alfred 'reading' the Saxon book to his mother, the story of Alfred's invention of the horn lantern, the story of

Alfred's scolding his nobles and officials because they had not learned to read, and so on. These stories seem rather to belong to tradition and folklore than to hard contemporary fact, indeed they are very much of a piece with 'Alfred and the Cakes', though that in fact is not among them. Finally there is in chapters 79–81 an autobiography of Asser, who tells us how he was summoned from Wales, and of the splendid gifts he received from the king. Three later chapters (87–89) describe how he taught Alfred to read and translate on one and the same day, having already put together for the king's use a Handbook of choice passages from devotional works. Nowhere is there any attempt to describe the king's personal appearance; and the work, which is dedicated to the king, ends unfinished in the year 893, six years before Alfred's death.

How should one tackle this problem? There are (it seems to me) two guiding principles to be borne in mind.

1. We must take up the problem from the point reached by previous writers, measure their assured results and build upon their work. The whole progress of knowledge depends upon this obligation to discuss a problem in the context of earlier inquiry. This done, it may be necessary to examine the question *de novo*, and possibly even from a new angle. But first our debt must be paid to our predecessors, so that the reader can judge at the end what advance, if any, has been made in the discussion. To start in on any problem in total disregard of past inquiry is essentially dishonest, and muddies the stream of growing knowledge.

2. We must try to be impartial in our weighing of the evidence, and objective in our criticism. In particular we must distinguish carefully between the subjective judgment (our personal opinion) and objective matters of fact.

# WHO WROTE ASSER'S LIFE OF ALFRED?

IN the *Quarterly Review* (July 1904) F. W. Maitland,[1] reviewing Liebermann's edition of the Anglo-Saxon Laws, remarked that 'Asser was supremely fortunate in the hands of Mr Stevenson'. He was referring to *Asser's Life of Alfred* published by the Clarendon Press in the same year, which first established the original text of the single manuscript, unfortunately destroyed in the Cottonian fire (1731). First published by Archbishop Parker in 1574, with various insertions from other manuscripts, it was reprinted by Camden in 1602–3 with the famous addition of the passage about Oxford University, republished in 1722 by Francis Wise, and finally reissued by Henry Petrie in the *Monumenta Historica Brittannica* (1848). To a text of rather under a hundred pages, Stevenson wrote a Preface of more than a hundred pages together with a commentary of two hundred pages, to which after sixty years there is not a great deal to be added. He concluded that

although there may be no very definite proof that the work was written by Bishop Asser in the lifetime of King Alfred, there is no anachronism or other proof that it is a spurious compilation of later date. The serious charges brought against its authenticity break down altogether under examination, while there remain several features that point with varying strength to the conclusion that it is, despite its difficulties and corruptions, really a work of the time it purports to be.[2]

It is worth remarking that in coming to this conclusion Stevenson was to a great extent preaching to the already

[1] *Collected Papers*, III, p. 459.
[2] p. vii.

converted, at any rate in England. The most serious attacks upon its authenticity, those of Thomas Wright in 1841, and Henry Howorth (1876–7), had already failed to shake the faith of the classic writers such as Freeman, Stubbs, and Maitland, and today their successors, sustained by Stevenson's masterpiece, have accepted the book as Asser's 'very naïve but sincerely intimate biography'.[1] And yet here and there doubts persist; and I interpret the successive withdrawal of two well-equipped scholars from their initial undertaking to edit the book for Nelson's *Medieval Texts* as indicative of a certain shift of critical feeling in the half-century that has elapsed since Stevenson wrote. In his recent edition of the *Chronicle of Aethelweard*, Professor Alistair Campbell remarks

Yet whether the biography is by Asser or by an eleventh-century Welsh scholar, its main importance is that it gives us a translation of an important section of an otherwise unknown version of OEC.[2]

In view of this expert judgment it is, perhaps, permissible to reconsider Stevenson's conclusions in the light of the evidence he himself so fully supplies. Nor should we forget the last paragraph of Stevenson's Introduction in which he says that 'the failure of the attacks upon the authenticity of the Life of Alfred must not, however, blind us to the difficulties it presents.'[3] Of these the most serious in his opinion was c. 74 which contains an improbable and fantastic account of Alfred's various diseases. 'Much may be forgiven to Celtic rhetoric,' wrote Stevenson, 'but one

---

[1] Stenton, *Anglo-Saxon England*, p. 268.
[2] *The Chronicle of Aethelweard* (Nelson's Medieval Texts), ed. A. Campbell, p. xxxiii. OEC: Old English Chronicle, the term used to cover all versions of the Anglo-Saxon Chronicle. [3] p. cxxix.

G

cannot help wondering what the "truth-telling" King would have thought of such exaggerations or misrepresentations.'[1] One cannot indeed: and the reader who takes the trouble to master the whole book will encounter other grave doubts which underlay the editor's final verdict. He may feel that the whole book is a sustained rearguard action in which every difficulty is looked firmly in the face, and then not so much explained, as explained away. He may even conclude, as I do, that Stevenson's own presentation of the evidence justifies a contrary verdict.

Between the two hundred pages of annotation and the Introduction to Stevenson's book there is a slight but unmistakable difference of tone. The notes examine objectively every difficulty and bear repeated witness to the editor's sense of their gravity. In the Introduction, evidently written last, when his mind was made up, he is at once more outspoken and dogmatic in his defence of the Life. The evidence of the notes is given a 'new look' in the Introduction. Only, then, from the annotation can we realise how deep-seated his own suspicions had been: nor is it irrelevant to add that his final summing-up of the evidence in his Introduction has never justified the easy assurance with which later scholars have used the Life.

It is proposed to set out below a new and positive hypothesis regarding the date and authorship of the Life, which largely rests upon the basic conclusions which Stevenson himself laid down. First, he proved clearly that the author must have been a Welshman, or at least a Cornishman. Secondly, he showed that the author's over-rhetorical prose was so deeply coloured by Frankish Latinity as to

---

[1] p. cxxx.

suggest that he had been educated on the Continent.[1] Why this should be so, if indeed Asser was the author, it is hard to say, for there is no reason to think that his travels took him further abroad than England; nor does Stevenson attempt any explanation.[2] Thirdly, Stevenson rightly concluded that the entire Life, as it existed in the Cottonian manuscript, was the work of a single author. All theories of a contemporary substratum, later amplified, break down in the face of the author's distinctive and individual vocabulary. Thus in venturing upon a new interpretation we shall still be arguing from Stevenson's own premises.

Stevenson's final criterion of authenticity was the absence of any manifest anachronism. 'In the course of a microscopical examination of the work', he writes, 'we have failed to discover anything that can be called an anachronism.' His own book, however, suggests that it would be truer to say that there *may be* quite a number, but that in our unfathomable ignorance of the ninth century none can be positively demonstrated. And yet, is this quite true? Take, for example, the Dedication with which the Life begins

To my venerable and most pious lord, ruler of all christians of the island of Britain.

This is nonsense. Alfred was never ruler of all the Christians of the island of Britain. But why did the author write it? The answer is simple. He wrote it because he had already in the text of his book mistranslated the entry in the

---

[1] p. xciii.
[2] Nevertheless, in his note (p. 286) on the eclipse mentioned in c.59, he supposes the author to have been on the Continent, and at no great distance from Fulda when it occurred, 'since we can scarcely doubt that the specification of time given by him is derived from personal observation'.

Chronicle for the year 886. The Chronicle says that in this year Alfred occupied London and

All the English people submitted to him, except those who were in captivity to the Danes.

The author of the Life mistranslated this entry as follows,

In this year Alfred occupied London, and all the Angles and Saxons, who had formerly been dispersed or in captivity to the Danes, voluntarily submitted themselves to Alfred's dominion.

And this is exactly what the Dedication says. It is not a mere rhetorical flourish. The author was serious and believed it. But how could he have gone so far wrong on a contemporary event that happened when he was living at Alfred's court? It is as though a man living in England in 1940 did not know who won the Battle of Britain. But worse is to follow. The Dedication continues

To my venerable and most pious lord, ruler of all the Christians of the island of Britain, Alfred, King of the Anglo-Saxons.[1]

A dozen times Alfred is referred to as Rex Angulsaxonum in the Life. For the author it clearly represented the formal 'style', or title of the king. This, again, is nonsense. There is plenty of evidence that Alfred's style was 'King of the West Saxons'. That Alfred changed his title after 886 is scarcely credible: nor does Stevenson venture to assert that any such change was made. What he does say in effect is that if the work is genuine it cannot be later than the middle of the tenth century, since the royal style was certainly *Rex Anglorum* after that date—thus assuming what he had set out to prove. Nor is this acceptable. For the barbarous compound *rex Angulsaxonum* was one made by history, when men looked back to the late ninth

[1] *Anglorum Saxonum:* but in later references in the text *rex Angulsaxonum*.

century, for which no original royal charters survived: and its *floruit* lies not in the early but in the late tenth and eleventh centuries, and above all in the twelfth when it was seized upon by the forgers of charters. In this connexion it is of interest to note that in the charter of 1001, the writing of which was said by Wanley to resemble that of the Cottonian manuscript, King Aethelred is actually described as *rex et rector Angul Saxne*.[1] Indeed, so uncertain is the evidence that no diplomatist would commit himself to the opinion that any king ever bore the royal style of *Rex Angulsaxonum*. In the light of these considerations there is an overwhelming probability that the Dedication contains one error only explainable on the assumption that the writer lived long after the time of which he was writing, and one anachronism which fixes that time as the eleventh century.

More damning, if possible, is a second anachronism, that to me seems irreconcilable with the facts and demands a closer scrutiny than it receives either in Stevenson's notes or in his Introduction. I refer to 'Asser's' statement in c. 81 that King Alfred gave him Exeter together with the whole diocese (*parochia*) that belonged to it in Saxony and in Cornwall. The very notion of a bishopric at Exeter at this date arouses our suspicions, unless, with Dr Finberg, we entirely discount the evidence of William of Malmesbury. However that may be, all Stevenson is able to prove[2] is

[1] *Facsimiles of Anglo-Saxon Charters in the British Museum*, Vol. iv, No. 12.
[2] See pp. 321–3, where Stevenson summarises the varying interpretations of this passage given by Haddan, Lingard and Freeman. For Dr Finberg's views see *Trans. Royal Hist. Soc.*, (5), iii, 1953, pp. 115 sqq. Dr Finberg believes that Asser received the monastery of Exeter in which St Boniface had been educated, while acting as *chorepiscopus* to the bishop of Sherborne in Devon and Cornwall. In the absence of any positive evidence the studied ambiguity of Asser's language leaves room for almost any hypothesis.

that it would have been within the bounds of possibility for the King to have made Asser bishop of Devonshire and Cornwall. That he ever did so there is not a shred of evidence—not even a tradition—apart from the Life. But that is not what 'Asser' says. He claims to have been made bishop of Exeter, a see only created in 1050, when bishop Leofric (1046–72), with papal permission, moved his see from near-by Crediton. We are asked to believe that in so doing history was repeating itself, or that he was repeating history. Stevenson was, of course, alive to all this and remarks in his note

This portion of the Life was written in a hand some fifty years or so older than this date, a fact that puts out of court the attempts that have been made to prove that the work is a forgery of a later date than the removal of the see to Exeter.[1]

The only serious evidence for the date of the Cottonian MS is that of Wanley who wrote that the

Cottonian Asser is not written by one hand, but by several, and much about the same time. The beginning is of the best and stanchest hand and seems to have been written about A.D. 1000. My authority for adjusting the age of that exemplar is an original charter of King Aethelred dated 1001, which as to the hand, agreeth very well with the first part of Asser, Otho A. 12.[2]

This is all right as far as it goes, but in the past half-century

[1] p. 321.
[2] *Review of English Studies*, 7, 1931, p. 8, footnote 4. See Plate XX, the so-called 'facsimile' of f. 1 of the Cottonian MS. In my opinion only wishful thinking could induce anyone to date the Cottonian MS as 'late 10th or early 11th century' on the strength of this poor freehand copy. It should also be noted that the O.E. land-books are very doubtful criteria for dating MSS since they bore no certain marks of authentication, such as seals or autograph signatures. It is therefore only an assumption that any particular charter was written at the time indicated by the dating clause. Moreover c. 89–98 are stated by Wise to have been written '*manu recentiori*'.

palaeographers have lost the simple faith of the Victorians in the exact dating of manuscripts by their script alone, and with no manuscript before us it would be unwise to attempt a closer dating than about the first half of the century. Nor, of course, does the mention of Exeter require a date after 1050 for the composition of the Life. It could be that the Life was written by someone connected with the diocese of Crediton anxious to have it moved to Exeter. The purpose of the move when it occurred in 1050 was to secure greater protection from piratical raids, and the idea of it may well have dated from the union of the sees of Crediton and Cornwall under bishop Lyfing in 1027, or indeed any date later than the refortification of the city by Athelstan. The mention of Exeter in the Life could even be a deliberate anachronism, revealing the motive or one of the motives for its compilation. The very word Exeter, which could so easily have been avoided, looks deliberate.

This possibility is closely connected with the author's reference to Banwell and Congresbury in the same chapter, which in translation runs as follows

Then, at last, when I had resolved to demand leave absolutely, at dusk on the eve of the day of the Nativity of the Lord, I was summoned to him. And he handed to me two letters, in which was a detailed account of all things which were in two monasteries, called in the Saxon tongue, Congresbury and Banwell. On the same day he gave to me those two monasteries with all that was in them, and a pall of silk most precious, and as much incense as could be borne by a strong man. And he added these words, 'I do not give you these small things because I will not come to give you greater gifts.'

And, indeed, as time went on, he gave to me, to my surprise, Exeter, with the whole see (parochia) thereof in the land of the Saxons and in Cornwall, in addition to countless daily gifts of all manner of earthly goods, which it would be tedious to mention here, lest I try the patience of my readers. But let none think that it is from any vain glory, or in flattery, or from a desire for gaining greater honour, that I have called to mind so many gifts in this place. For I witness before God that not for such cause have I done this, but that I might make clear to those who know it not how bountiful is his generosity.[1]

This very circumstantial story (which is not made any better by the quotation from Einhard[2]) carries with it a further suggestion of anachronism by its inclusion of Banwell and Congresbury among the royal gifts. Long ago Stubbs remarked[3] in connexion with this passage, 'There were many monasteries standing empty in Asser's time', and on its authority concluded that 'monasticism for good or for evil was extinct before the reign of Alfred'. It may reasonably be doubted whether monasteries ever have or could have 'stood empty', like so many suburban villas. Nor (I think) did Asser mean to say so. His views on the matter are set out in c. 93 where he explains that at this time only children would submit to the full monastic life, although there were still many monasteries, none of which, however, was following the rule of that life in a regular manner.[4] This means in fact that the state of things brought to light at the time of the Dunstan revival was already in force. There were still plenty of religious houses, but they were no longer strictly monastic, so Alfred had to import foreign monks. Indeed the continued existence of the monasteries in Alfred's reign, whatever their

---

[1] Asser, *Life of King Alfred*, ed. by L. C. Jane (1908), p. 63.

[2] Pp. 107, below sqq.

[3] *Historical Introductions to the Rolls Series*, ed. A. Hassall, p. 369, n. 4. Cf. Stenton, *Anglo-Saxon England*, p. 268: 'it is probable that Alfred writing in 894, heavily over painted the depression of English learning in 871. He certainly did less than justice to the scholarship of that time.'

[4] 'Nullo tamen regulam illius vitae ordinabiliter tenente.'

personnel, is vouched for by Alfred's Laws, where, if there is not much about monks, there is a good deal about nuns. 'Asser's' remarks about Banwell and Congresbury, read alongside those in c. 93, carry the clear suggestion that the Life was written at some date after the tenth century revival. The decay of the monastic life in the previous century could hardly have been so well understood except in retrospect, when once more the monasteries were following the regular life.

In harmony with this conclusion is the surviving evidence regarding these two places. Nothing whatever is known about them as *monasteria* at any date. Both have left faint traces[1] in our early history, but their first clear appearance is in the eleventh century, and when they do appear, they are already conjoined. For according to a written statement by Giso,[2] bishop of Wells, they had been given to Wells Cathedral by Duduc, his predecessor (1033–60), who had received them from Edward the Confessor. Here again we are asked to believe that history had repeated itself, so that what was given to Duduc in the eleventh century, had previously been granted to Asser in the ninth. Moreover a particular significance attached to Congresbury in the eleventh century as the traditional site of the see of Somerset until bishop Daniel moved it to Wells. What then would an eleventh-century ecclesiastic

[1] Dr Finberg kindly informs me that the name Congresbury implies the presence of an ancient Celtic church of St Congar, and that his shrine is mentioned in the list of Resting-Places of the Saints, c. A.D. 1000. Banwell too is mentioned among the possessions of the See of Winchester in Birch's *Cart. Sax.* 612 (cf. CS. 12, 19–20) with the added information that Edward the Elder gave Compton and Banwell to the minster at Cheddar. These references, Dr Finberg adds, correct Stevenson's statement (p. 321) that 'nothing is known' of these churches before 1061.

[2] *Ecclesiastical Documents*, ed. Joseph Hunter (Camden Society, 1840), p. 15.

infer from Asser's statement? No less, surely, than that Asser had already been made bishop of Somerset, before the see of Exeter was added to him.

Thus in the course of a vague narrative of how Asser came to Alfred 'from the uttermost western parts of Britain' at a place unknown and at a time unspecified we encounter a precise list of the king's gifts to him, which imply that he was made bishop of Somerset, Exeter and Cornwall. Add to this that Asser is nowhere called bishop of Sherborne in the Life, and we are left with the plain inference that after his accession to the see of Sherborne (the only definite fact known about him[1]), he lived and died bishop of all England west of Winchester.[2]

Here then we have a plausible hypothesis that the Life was written in the first half of the eleventh century by some patriotic Welshman anxious to promote the removal of the see of Crediton to Exeter by suggesting that Asser had been bishop of Exeter long ago, as well as the whole of the west of England. In the tenth century, following the respite gained by Alfred's stubborn resistance to the Danes, many new sees were created in Wessex, and the idea of having a bishop to each shire seems to have been in the mind of their creator.[3] This reorganisation was of the

[1] King Alfred refers to him as 'Asserie minum biscepe' (in the dative case) in the Preface to his translation of the *Pastoral Care* as one of his helpers.

[2] In addition to the supposed grant of Banwell, Congresbury and Exeter, there are other 'difficulties' connected with chapters 79–81 of the Life, e.g. Nobis is described as archbishop of St David's, and in c. 79, l. 33, Wintonia has to be interpreted not as a reference to Winchester (as elsewhere in the Life) but as Caerwent in Wales to save Asser's credit. His terminology is, understandably, so vague as to make it unprofitable to discuss the meaning he attached either to the word *parochia* or *monasterium*. St David's is a *monasterium*, Banwell and Congresbury are *monasteria*, while Exeter is just Exeter.

[3] Stubbs, *Const. Hist.*, i. 259; *Crawford Charters*, ed. Napier and Stevenson, no. vii.

greatest interest to churchmen from the time of Dunstan onwards, and gave rise to much confused speculation; but our evidence, such as it is, assigns this activity to the reign of Edward the Elder, the *terminus a quo* being the year 909. Beyond that date memory does not seem to have stretched. What more likely than that an eleventh-century writer should have pushed this *terminus* rather further back?

It is in accordance with Stevenson's own conclusions that the author should be a Welshman. But Stevenson also called attention both to the writer's knowledge of foreign sources and to the strong influence of Frankish Latin upon his vocabulary. Can we go further and find an eleventh-century Welshman, educated in foreign parts, who was closely interested in the removal of the see of Crediton to Exeter? We have not far to look: for bishop Leofric,[1] who in fact moved the see to Exeter, was himself a Welshman, *altus et doctus* among the Lotharingians, and seems to have been brought to England by Edward the Confessor. He performed the duties of the later chancellor and was rewarded successively with a gift of land at Dawlish (1044) and the bishopric of Crediton (1046). He was an energetic prelate, travelling widely and preaching in Devonshire and Cornwall, and four years later, after application to Rome, he moved the see to the walled city of Exeter because of the barbaric attacks of the pirates. Both the king and queen attended his enthronement as the first bishop of Exeter.[2]

The hypothesis that Leofric was responsible for the Life of Alfred in the form in which it was preserved in the Cottonian manuscript finds strong, if unexpected, support

---

[1] *The Exeter Book*, ed. Chambers, Förster and Flower, p. 5. For Leofric's bequest ibid., pp. 18 sqq.

[2] 'Primus episcopus factus est Exoniensis' (Monasticon, II. 526).

in the construction put by Dr Finberg on the facts summarised above. He points out that an episcopal see in Cornwall was established by King Aethelred in 994, who gave it full episcopal jurisdiction. This ecclesiastical autonomy, however, only lasted until the year 1027 when Cnut allowed bishop Lyfing to hold both sees in plurality. This uncanonical privilege was again extended by Edward the Confessor to bishop Leofric (1046), who, having first transferred the Devonshire see to Exeter with papal approval, is stated to have then secured a charter from Edward the Confessor amalgamating the two bishoprics of Devon and Cornwall.

It cannot be taken for granted [writes Dr Finberg], that the Pope would have agreed to this amalgamation, if he had been asked. The evidence suggests that he had been neatly circumvented. For pluralism, then as now the obvious expedient for a church in financial straits, was prohibited by canon law; and by this union of bishoprics Leofric had ceased to be a pluralist. With that stigma removed, and with his see established in an urban centre, his position was canonically unimpeachable.[1]

Here, surely, we have a convincing and practical motive for asserting in the Life that the two sees had already been united in Alfred's reign under bishop Asser. It is moreover a motive that harmonises with the somewhat crooked manœuvres which Dr Finberg attributes to Leofric.

Thus Leofric fulfils all the conditions required for authorship: and, as though for full measure, still further and exciting evidence is supplied by Leofric's famous bequest of books to his cathedral. Among these were

Sedulius' *Carmen Paschale*.
Gregory I's *Pastoral Care*.

[1] *Trans. Royal Hist. Soc.*, 5, iii, 1953, pp. 120-1.

Boethius' *Consolation of Philosophy*, both in the original Latin and in Alfred's English translation.
Gregory I's *Dialogues*.
A volume (unspecified) of Prosper of Aquitaine.
The *Liber Oserii*.

Taking these in order we find that the author of the Life included a long quotation from Sedulius in chapter 1. Gregory's *Pastoral Care* was one of the books translated by Alfred, who acknowledges in the Preface the help of Asser, his bishop. It is also quoted in c. 102 of the Life. Boethius' *Consolation of Philosophy* was also translated by Alfred, who in the Preface says that he has translated it sometimes word for word, and sometimes sense by sense. According to William of Malmesbury Asser explained to the king the difficult passages in the work and the king made his translation from this simplified version: but the king in his Preface makes no mention of Asser's assistance. According to the Life (c. 77) Gregory's *Dialogues* were translated from Latin into English by Werfrith, bishop of Worcester, who at times made his rendering most elegantly 'sense by sense'. There may be some confusion here, and it is at least likely that the author of the Life had read the preface to the *Consolation of Philosophy*. As for Prosper's book, it is no more than a guess that it may have included the quotation from St Augustine in c. 103.

There remains the *Liber Oserii*, which Max Förster has suggested may have been a copy of the Life. The evidence is inconclusive and the best argument in its favour is that the book is otherwise totally unknown to medieval catalogues. There is, too, no doubt about the title, for it occurs again in a fourteenth-century Exeter catalogue, with the opening words of f. 2. These are not found in the Life, but may belong to another work within the same cover. It may then be that the work refers to Asser, although not necessarily a copy of the Life. It could quite well have been Alfred's Handbook which is more than once quoted by William of Malmesbury, or the *Dicta Alfredi* to which Florence of Worcester has a reference. The important point is that it does seem to refer by name to Bishop Asser.

Here then we have a not inconsiderable fraction of the literary sources used in the Life. The absence of Einhard and the Anglo-Saxon Chronicle—which could be deliberate—does not detract from the significance of so many other necessary books, and it is important to remember that under a single title several works may be included. From this list, too, we gain some indication of the limitations of the author's knowledge. He knows about and uses the relevant books in his library, but he knows nothing of the translations of Bede, or Orosius, or the Soliloquies of St Augustine. He even got mixed up in using Boethius, and he did not know that Asser was mentioned in Alfred's Preface to the *Pastoral Care*, because he had only the Latin text.

Such are the grounds for attributing the Life to bishop Leofric. The hypothesis, of course, could be and perhaps should be widened to include the possibility that the actual author was an ecclesiastic in Leofric's service, or a Crediton colleague; and, so qualified, seems to me to have strong claims on our acceptance. The evidence, even if largely circumstantial, is many-sided, and provides both an intelligible motive for the forgery and an explanation of why it ends unfinished. The author of the Life, like Nennius before him and the fraudulent Geoffrey of Monmouth afterwards, was a Welshman. And in eulogising King Alfred he also glorified Wales in the person of Asser, whom he could not resist making bishop both of Somerset

and of his own see of Exeter! Such a motive is characteristic of a medieval literary forger, and the Life, we
may recall here, was written in the very heyday of forgery.
To the medieval mind it was rather an innocent imposture
which gave added dramatic and literary force to the Life.
Not that it deceived medieval writers, who, with unerring
instinct, extracted every historical fact, ignoring the
passages which identified the author with Bishop Asser.[1]
All that is of value, and it is a great deal, was embodied in
the chronicles of Symeon of Durham and Florence of
Worcester, and the Annals of St Neot's. Florence's extracts
were used in the works of William of Malmesbury, who
lived and died entirely unaware that Asser had written a
life of Alfred. His ignorance was shared by later writers;
and it was only in the age of enlightenment, when the
work was printed from the Cottonian MS by Archbishop
Parker (1574), that historians began to take it seriously.
The Life, as such, was virtually unknown in the Middle
Ages, and its fame is post-medieval.

## II

The Life, then, like so many medieval documents, has a
betwixt-and-between character—half true and half false.
Such a conception was foreign to the sturdy Victorian
scholars who saw the problem as a simple alternative: was
it genuine or was it the 'spurious' work of a 'forger'? In
fact it is at once both more complicated and more subtle:
nor need this occasion any surprise in an age when most
historical writing contained a large admixture of legend,
folklore, hearsay, and mere wishful thinking. As a biography of Alfred the Life is substantially genuine, using

[1] Both Florence and William of Malmesbury believed that Asser died
in 883!

the Anglo-Saxon Chronicle and quite possibly other written sources. But in so far as it is an autobiography of Asser, it is pure fiction. The famous chapters 79, 81, 88, and 89 which purport to describe in detail Asser's personal relations with the king are mere invention, although c. 80, which admirably summarises the history of Wales during the reign, rests upon sources which have largely survived in the twelfth-century manuscript of the *Liber Landavensis*. There are in addition a dozen or more passages peppered through the book which emphasise Asser's personal knowledge of the events he describes, which long ago excited the suspicions of Charles Plummer[1] and are equally imaginary. Thus in c. 13 a highly improbable story is introduced by the remark that the author had often heard the king tell it on the authority of unimpeachable witnesses. In c. 15 the sad end of Eadburh, living in poverty and misery with only a single attendant, is 'proved' by the statement that the author had heard the story from many who had seen her. The site of the great battle of 871 (c. 39) was marked by a single thorn tree 'quam nos ipsi nostris propriis oculis vidimus', and he is equally familiar with the (unknown) site of Cynuit 'sicut nos ipsi vidimus'. By these and similar instances[2] he seeks to impress the personality of Asser upon the narrative; but he protests too much and too often and all can confidently be excised.

The real problem is to discover how this curious result came about. What suggested the idea of telling the story through the mouth of bishop Asser? The 'big idea' could have been a stroke of Celtic genius on the author's part; but it is more likely that the device was borrowed from another and more famous source. Some years after the

---

[1] *Life and Times of Alfred the Great* (Clarendon Press, 1902), pp. 15–17.
[2] e.g. c. 29, ll. 8–10; c. 37, l. 13.

death of Charlemagne, Einhard, who had lived in his household, and refers to him as his 'nutritor', wrote a life of his benefactor which began as follows:

Vitam et conversationem et ex parte non modica res gestas domini et nutritoris mei Karoli, excellentissimi et merito famosissimi regis, postquam scribere animus tulit, quanta potui brevitate conplexus sum, operam inpendens ut de his quae ad meam notitiam pervenire potuerunt nihil omitterem neque prolixitate narrandi nova quaeque fastidientium animos offenderem, si tamen hoc ullo modo vitari potest ut nova scriptione non offendantur qui vetera et a viris doctissimis atque disertissimis confecta monumenta fastidiunt.[1]

In c. 73 of 'Asser' the author interrupts his translation of the Chronicle to explain his purpose in undertaking the work. It is the same as that of Einhard, and expressed in his very words

Igitur, ut ad id, unde digressus sum, redeam, ne diuturna enaviga-tione portum optatae quietis omittere cogar, aliquantulum, *quantum notitiae meae innotuerit, de vita et moribus et aequa conversatione*, atque, *ex parte non modica*, res gestas domini mei Aelfredi, Angulsaxonum regis, postquam praefatam ac venerabilem de Merciorum nobilium genere coniugem duxerit, Deo annuente, succinctim ac *breviter, ne qua prolixitate narrandi nova quaeque fastidientium animos offendam*, ut promisi, expedire procurabo.[2]

---

[1] Eginhard, *Vie de Charlemagne*, ed. Halphen, p. 1. 'I have decided to set down, as briefly as I can, a description of the life and character of my lord Charles, and of at least the principal events of his reign; for he was a most excellent and deservedly famous king, and I was educated in his household. I shall not leave out anything that I know: but at the same time I shall hope not to try the patience of those who have no use for anything modern—though it is a forlorn hope for a modern author to hope to please an audience that has no use even for the classics.'

[2] The italics, which are my own, show how closely Einhard is followed in this passage. 'And so to return to the point, because otherwise my story will never reach harbour. As I promised, I am going to tell you what little I know about the life, habits and character of my lord Alfred, king of the Anglo-Saxons, and at least the principal events of his reign. I shall start from

The *ut promisi* (as I promised) is meaningless, for nowhere in the preceding narrative has he made such a promise. He seems, however, to have referred to it earlier in c. 21, where he had already written

Sed, ut more navigantium loquar, ne diutius navim undis et velamentis concedentes, et a terra longius enavigantes longum circumferamur inter tantas bellorum clades et annorum enumerationes, ad id, quod nos maxime ad hoc opus incitavit, nobis redeundum esse censeo, scilicet aliquantulum, quantum meae cognitioni innotuit, de infantilibus et puerilibus domini mei venerabilis Aelfredi, Angulsaxonum regis, moribus hoc in loco breviter inserendum esse existimo.[1]

This passage, which also echoes the words of Einhard, was no doubt suggested by c. 4 of the Life of Charlemagne. There Einhard explains that he cannot, alas, write anything 'de nativitate atque infantia vel etiam pueritia'[2] of his hero, as no one survived who knew of them when he was writing. Regarding Alfred's childhood, therefore, 'Asser' is ready to out-Einhard Einhard!

In addition, there are two other places in which 'Asser's' words recall those of Einhard. In c. 16 he writes—

Nam cetera, quae ad humanam dispensationem pertinent, in hoc

---

the time when he married my lady his wife, whom I have mentioned before, and who came of a noble Mercian family. I shall try, with God's help, to be brief, hoping not to try the patience of those who have no use for anything modern.'

[1] 'But I will no longer run before the wind, as sailors say, nor drift out of sight of land amidst a waste of carnage and chronology. No, I will return to my original subject. I shall set down briefly all that I know, little as it is, about the habits of my revered lord Alfred, king of the Anglo-Saxons, in his infancy and boyhood.'

[2] '. . . about the birth and infancy or even about the boyhood . . .'

opusculo inserere necesse non est, *ne fastidium prolixitate legentibus* vel etiam audire desiderantibus procreaverit.[1]

and again in c. 81, quoted above (p. 95)

exceptis cotidianis donis innumerabilibus in omni genere terrestris divitiae, quae hoc in loco percensere longum est, *ne fastidium legentibus procreent.*

With these borrowings before us, it is a reasonable assumption that in the many passages in 'Asser' in which the author claims to have been present at events or to have spoken to eyewitnesses, or to have seen the places, he has in mind Einhard's claim to have been an eyewitness of what he describes

tamen ab hujuscemodi scriptione non existimavi temperandum' quando mihi conscius eram nullum ea veracius quam me scribere posse, quibus ipse interfui quaeque praesens oculata, ut dicunt, fide cognovi et utrum ab alio scriberentur necne liquido scire non potui.[2]

These various references to Einhard show that his influence upon the author of 'Asser' went deeper than Stevenson had thought, though he characteristically noted that in the chapters immediately following c. 73

We can perceive some indications that the order of his biographical matter has been influenced by that in Einhard.[3]

It has indeed, and more than ten years ago I wrote of 'Asser's' Life

Why indeed was it ever written? The answer, I think, is in no doubt.

---

[1] 'It is not necessary to include in this work the provisions which concern his temporal estate, lest I try the patience of those who read it or would like to hear it read.'

[2] 'However, I have not refrained from writing this book, because I know that no one can describe more accurately than I events at which I was present and which I saw, as they say, "with these very eyes".'

[3] p. lxxxi.

The author drew his inspiration from Einhard's *Life of Charlemagne*, with whose achievement he rightly felt Alfred would bear comparison. For not only does he actually quote from Einhard's preface (with two other side allusions) but his whole book is really an English echo of its exemplar. Alfred's love of Saxon poems, his skill in hunting, his devotion to the 'liberal arts', especially reading and writing both for himself and his children, his wars, his alms to Rome and to poor Christians everywhere, his justice, his division of his revenue—for all these we have precedents and parallels in Einhard.[1]

This pervasive indebtedness to Einhard disguised as it is by the barbarous Latinity of 'Asser', had already raised doubts in my mind, for it justified a presumption that the work could scarcely have been compiled earlier than the eleventh century. It would never have occurred to anyone in the ninth century that the two men were of comparable importance. Wessex was still on the defensive when Alfred died, and its very survival was not yet assured in 893. It required not only the conquests of the tenth century, but also the collapse that followed the renewed Scandinavian invasions to demonstrate the greatness of Alfred's work. The growing reputation of Alfred is first attested in the late tenth century by the chronicle of Aethelweard,[2] who of course knew nothing of the Life. The work was undertaken for his relative Matilda, Alfred's great-grand-

---

[1] *Historical Research in Mediaeval England* (Athlone Press, 1951), p. 13.

[2] *The Chronicle of Aethelweard* (Nelson's Medieval Texts), ed. A. Campbell. Aethelweard had no knowledge of a chronicle written by bishop Asser, and his silence, as Howorth argued long ago, is only to be explained by the fact that the Life had not yet been written. Stevenson's description of Aethelweard's chronicle as 'merely a brief version of the history of England, with no personal details, drawn up from the Chronicle which supplied in abundance all the material that he needed' (p. cxvii) is both false and disingenuous. It is even arguable that the author of 'Asser' made some slight use of Aethelweard.

daughter, while he himself was descended, he tells us, from Alfred's brother. Both were inordinately proud of their descent and Alfred's reign is the climax of the book. Later evidence of an Alfred cult is found in the rich growth of legend which associated his name with St Neot and St Cuthbert, in the 'Dicta regis Alfredi' and the 'Liber Manualis', which seem to have been works current in the eleventh century; in the legend of Alfred and the Cakes, which occurs in the Annals of St Neots, in others like it in William of Malmesbury; and in a large crop of forged charters purporting to belong to Alfred's reign. The use of Einhard by the author of the Life is a powerful argument for an eleventh-century date but I had not then realised the full significance of Einhard's life as the author's model. It was because the parallel between the relative situation of Einhard to Charlemagne and of Asser to Alfred was so exact, that the welsh author of 'Asser', writing in the eleventh century, wrote his book. Alfred had been, in effect, Asser's *nutritor*, and the latter had outlived his benefactor by ten years. Who could write of Alfred's boyhood and manhood better than the man who had taught him to read?[1] From this it was a short step to fathering the Life upon Asser, whose book thus became wholly analogous to that of Einhard.

To this conclusion there was one objection which seemed at first to be insuperable. Einhard had been written after Charlemagne's death: Asser's Life in 893, when Alfred had still six years to live. I was thus led to a minute

[1] With characteristic naïvety 'Asser' takes sole credit for teaching the king to read. Other foreign 'helpers' are mentioned in c. 77, whose doctrine and wisdom kindled the king's desire for knowledge and familiarised him with books. For these services they were richly rewarded, but the author is careful to add that the king was still unable to read anything until he (Asser) arrived from Wales.

examination of the actual text. In general it reads like the life of a man no longer alive. The king's habits and aspirations are described in the past tense: so much so that Stevenson had sought for and found a precedent in Thegan's *Life of Louis the Pious* which was completed while its subject was still alive. But Stevenson, with his usual thoroughness, has also called attention to what he described as 'a curious confusion of present and imperfect tenses in reference to Alfred'. There are a large number of instances, meticulously listed by Stevenson, in which the author begins by speaking of the king in the imperfect, and then suddenly and unaccountably changes to the present tense. These variations Stevenson most inadequately explained as due to the eleventh-century copyist of the Cottonian manuscript—inadequately because there was no reason why the copyist should have made such changes. 'The theory' he added[1]

that these imperfects are due to a forger who has momentarily forgotten that he ought not to speak of the King, in whose reign he professes to be writing, in the past tense, is difficult to reconcile with the numerous instances in which the imperfect occurs and with the frequency of the present. A forger would surely have corrected all or none of the verbs in his draught; he would not be likely to issue it to the world with these contradictions. The view that the imperfects are due to a transcriber who frequently omits to change the presents of the copy before him is much more probable.

These words of Stevenson are a good example both of the special pleading to which he was driven to defend the contemporaneity of the Life, and of the Victorian conception of 'the forger' as a very wicked but very, very clever man.[2] None the less, Stevenson here comes very near to

[1] p. l.
[2] e.g. p. lxxiii, 'It seems to us that a forger would not have committed

the true explanation, which is that the author began the Life on the assumption that he was writing of a dead king, and then, changing his plan at an advanced stage of the book, terminated it abruptly at the year 893. This involved an elaborate revision of the primitive text, of which ample traces remain. This evidence is summarised in the following examples of what we may fairly call the anarchy of tenses which characterised the final text of the Cottonian manuscript.

(*a*) In c. 22 the author tells us that Alfred remained illiterate until his twelfth year or later, and continues: Sed Saxonica poemata die noctuque solers auditor, relatu aliorum saepissime audiens, docibilis memoriter retinebat. [In omni venatoria arte industrius venator incessabiliter laborat non in vanum; nam incomparabilis omnibus peritia et felicitate in illa arte sicut et in ceteris omnibus Dei donis, fuit, sicut et nos saepissime vidimus.] Cum ergo . . .

Then follows the story of Alfred's mother promising the book of Saxon poems to whichever of her children could quickest learn it. The words in square brackets are clearly a later insertion by the author. They interrupt the sense of what precedes and what follows. They use the present tense (*laborat*); and their purpose is apparently to remind the reader that Alfred is still alive, and working away at his hunting, and so is the author who has so often seen him doing it.

(*b*) c. 25 begins
Quod maximum *inter omnia praesentis vitae suae impedimenta* et dispendia . . .

---

such a stupid blunder as this'; p. ciii, 'It is difficult to conceive a forger so stupid' and 'we must allow at least half a century before we can assume that a forger would be likely to make the mistake of calling Asser bishop of Exeter in the ninth century'. By pp. cv and cviii the forger has become 'the imaginary forger'.

Lines 2–12 then relate how Alfred used to say (*affirmabat*) that when he was young he had no masters to teach him, and later when masters were available, he was too busy and too ill to learn. Then:

Sed tamen *inter praesentis vitae impedimenta* ab infantia usque ad praesentem diem [et, ut credo, usque ad obitum vitae suae][1] in eodem insaturabili desiderio, sicut nec ante destituit, ita nec etiam adhuc inhiare desinit.

The repetition of the words in italics warns us of the coming insertion, which says, in effect, that he has loved learning from infancy: he still loves it now and will continue to do so till the day of his death. The use of the imperfect tense in the primitive text had implied that the king was already dead when the author wrote.

(*c*) c. 92 described the foundation of Athelney abbey in which Alfred placed foreign monks. It ends: in quo monasterio diversi generis monachos undique congregavit et in eodem collocavit.

C. 94 which begins with the statement that its first abbot was John the Old Saxon follows naturally from the concluding phrase of c. 92. Into this original text the author appears to have inserted c. 93, which explains the decay of the monastic life, although, he adds, there are still in existence (*permaneant*) a great number of monasteries which are no longer following the strict rule, whether because of the constant attacks the enemy are making by land and sea, or because of the too great abundance of riches, he is unable to decide. All this is in the present tense

---

[1] The words in square brackets were stigmatised by Stevenson as an interpolation made in order 'to bring the information down to the time of the Cottonian MS.' I am unable to understand why a copyist should have wished to do this. In any case, the excision is unwarranted, the phrase '*usque ad obitum vitae suae*' having previously been used by the author in c. 13.

and the inserted chapter ends with the repetition of the closing phrase of c. 92:

ideo diversi generis monachos in eodem monasterio congregare studuit.

In (b) and (c) the passages inserted by the author strike the eye from the repetition of a key phrase, and the sudden transition from the past tense of the original text to the present of the insertions. There are, besides these, many other passages in which the sudden use of the present tense suggests that they are insertions. These changes have complicated the narrative and go far towards explaining Stevenson's strictures on the text—its confused order, the cloud of verbiage which often obscures the meaning, its unmethodical habit of anticipating events and then returning suddenly to the theme from which it has wandered away. There is truth, of course, in Stevenson's criticism, but it is not the whole truth, for a great deal of the original text is concise, clear and informative.[1]

(d) More complicated are the alterations and insertions in c. 74, the chapter describing Alfred's diseases. No chapter has done more to discredit Asser, for the hagiographical picture of Alfred as a neurotic invalid is irreconcilable with all we really know about him from the Chronicle and the prefaces to his translations, and to suppose that such a narrative was ever read by the king is pure absurdity. It bears clear marks of a late monastic origin, and not improbably a life of St Neot, whose name occurs in it.[2] This chapter moreover has clearly been revised and

[1] Cf. Dr Marie Schütt, 'The Literary Form of Asser's "Vita Alfredi"' (Eng. Hist. Review, lxxii, 1957).

[2] 'ad quandam ecclesiam orandi causa divertisset, in qua Sanctus Gueriir requiescit [et nunc etiam Sanctus Niot ibidem pausat']. The words in square brackets were regarded by Stevenson as an interpolation, 'because they

interpolated by the author. As it now stands, it is self-contradictory, first alleging that Alfred suffered from the *ficus* from infancy, and later that he acquired the disease by prayer in the flower of his youth, and realised that in no other way could he refrain from the sins of the flesh.[1] The original text, we conclude, had one of these accounts, into which the author clumsily interpolated the other. Once again the author's revision of his text is signalled by the repetition of a key phrase; for in line 9 we are told that Alfred suffered from his unknown disease from his twentieth to his fortieth year and more, and in l. 62 that it endured from his twentieth to his forty-fifth year. Into this long and already confused account of diseases, all couched in the past tense as of a man long dead, the author has inserted two passages in the present tense. The first of these follows the statement that on his wedding day Alfred, in the presence of all the people was suddenly stricken with a disease, and continues

Incognitum enim erat omnibus, qui tunc aderant, [et etiam hucusque cotidie cernentibus—quod, proh dolor! pessimum est, tantam diurnitatem a vigesimo aetatis suae anno usque quadragesimum, et eo amplius, annum per tanta annorum curricula incessanter protelasse]—unde talis dolor oriebatur.

The words in square brackets are an obvious insertion by the author in his original text. The second alteration in this

---

fitted in so badly with the context' and 'were awkwardly inserted'. But the MS abounds in awkward insertions by the author, and the sentence in which it occurs runs to fourteen lines! It may well be an interpolation by the author, but, if so, the variation of *requiescit* and *pausat* suggests that we must extend it to include the words *in qua Sanctus Gueriir requiescit*.

[1] See L. C. Jane's translation of the Life (King's Classics), p. 135, who conjectures that large portions of c. 74 are interpolations; but, if so, they were added by the author.

chapter is an addition of seven lines at the end (lines 64–70) saying, in effect, that the fear and horror of this disease, which he has suffered from, from his twentieth to his forty-fifth year, never *leaves* him, for it has made him feel that he *is* useless for practical affairs. But for these two insertions of clauses in the present tense, the whole narrative is set in the past, and both insertions are surely designed to correct this impression.

(*e*) in c. 75, the chapter describing Alfred's family and their education—all written in the past tense—ten lines (l. 21–31) have apparently been added at the end; for they substantially repeat what has already been said, to the effect that two of the children *are* not allowed to live lazily, but *are* kept at their books of psalms and poetry.

(*f*) c. 91 begins as follows

Erat itaque rex ille multis tribulationum clavis confossus, quamvis in regia potestate constitutus; [nam a vigesimo aetatis anno usque ad quadragesimum quintum annum, quem nunc agit, gravissima incogniti doloris infestatione incessanter fatigatur, ita ut ne unius quidem horae securitatem habeat, qua aut illam infirmitatem non sustineat aut sub illius formidine lugubriter prope constitutus non desperet] Preterea assiduis exterarum gentium infestationibus, quas sedulo terra marique sine ullius quieti temporis intervallo sustinebat, non sine materia inquietabatur.[1]

The clauses in square brackets, on the same theme as those quoted above in (*d*), are in the present tense and are clearly insertions by the author in his original text. The key statement that Alfred had suffered from his unknown disease from his twentieth to his forty-fifth year is repeated for the third time in the Life—a clear indication that it has

---

[1] There are indications of further insertions in the later part of this chapter, but the original text has been so much altered as to have now become unusually rhetorical and confused.

been interpolated, while the words *quem nunc agit* inform the reader that the book is being written in the year 893, and so announce the author's change of plan.

Collectively, these passages supply a rational explanation of the mixture of the past and present tenses in the Life. They are due neither to 'confusion', nor to the copyist of the Cottonian manuscript, but to the author's revision of his original text, which was first intended to be a complete life of the king. They justify the conclusion that, at some point in its composition, he changed the work into an unfinished biography of the still living Alfred; for they occur at those places in the narrative which seem most to treat of the king as already dead, and their object is to correct this impression. However clumsy, they are methodically done; they are characterised by the repetition of key phrases; and the last example quoted above says in effect that the author is writing in 893. We have, moreover, in the Dedication more than a hint of the point in his narrative at which the change of plan occurred. The book is dedicated to 'Alfred, King of the Anglo-Saxons, ruler of all the Christians of the island of Britain', which, as we have already seen, is not in accordance with the facts.[1]

Nothing in the Life worried Stevenson more than this strange dedication and he acutely noted that 'although the Life is dedicated to Alfred, he is not otherwise addressed in it'.[2] Having got so far, it is surprising that the reason escaped him. In its original form the Life must certainly have begun with a Preface, closely modelled upon that of Einhard. That this was so is apparent from the references to it in c. 21 and c. 73.[3] In each of these chapters the author remarks—in words which echo Einhard—that he must

---

[1] Above, p. 91.      [2] p. cxxxi.      [3] Above, p. 105.

redeem his promise to speak of the king's youth, life and deeds. No such promise is found in the text as we have it, so that both these references are now meaningless. This at once reminds us that the change-over from a life of Alfred (dead) to Alfred (still alive) involved deletions from the primitive text as well as additions. We can never know their full extent, but it is plain that the original Preface to the Life was among them, and that for it was substituted the present unconvincing dedication. Moreover the Dedication shows that the Life had been carried as far as the year 886, if not further, when the change was made. This conclusion that the present Dedication was substituted for the original Preface can only be resisted by needlessly exaggerating—as Stevenson does—the author's incapacity as a writer. Equally, the mistranslation of the Chronicle for 886 and the anachronistic title of *Rex Angul-Saxonum* can only be satisfactorily explained on the assumption that the Life was written in the eleventh century, to which the only known manuscript belonged.

The hypothesis advanced above thus depends upon three converging lines of inquiry.

1. The manuscript and, possibly, the deliberate anachronism of the author in referring to the diocese of Exeter, which is unknown to history until Leofric, bishop of Cornwall and Crediton (1046–72), transferred his Devonshire see to Exeter. This clue brought to light strong circumstantial evidence in favour of the view that Leofric, or perhaps a member of his *familia*, was the author of the Life, prompted by Welsh patriotism, or even possibly to provide evidence from the past for moving the see to Exeter. The idea of such a transfer may well have been in the air at any time after bishop

Lyfing in 1027 was permitted to hold the Cornwall and Devonshire bishoprics in plurality, if not even earlier still.

2. The dominating influence of Einhard's *Life of Charlemagne* upon the scope and treatment of the Life, which not only points clearly to an eleventh-century date for its composition, but also seems to have suggested the idea of fathering the work upon Leofric's episcopal Welsh predecessor, bishop Asser.

3. The evidence in the surviving text of the Life of a change of plan and a consequent revision of the original narrative. It was begun as a Life by 'Bishop Asser' writing, as Einhard had written, after the death of his subject; and at a late stage in its composition, changed to a strictly contemporary biography, stopping abruptly at the year 893.

Behind the demonstrable revision of the text, with which alone we are here concerned, there may well be earlier developments in the evolution of the Life. Its original basis seems to have been the translation of the Chronicle. Much of this has little or no bearing on the life of the king, and if we ignore the dedication, the first mention of the author occurs only in c. 13. The translation of the Chronicle is everywhere slightly embroidered and inflated, a certain amount of new historical material is incorporated, and there are many traditional stories. All this is written in reasonably straightforward Latin. But in sharp contrast with this basic material is the obscurity and repetitiveness of the text in c. 74, the hagiographical chapter about the king's illness, and in those parts of the Life which most show the influence of Einhard. It could well be then that the work was begun as an ordinary, eleventh-century life

of Alfred by Leofric (or someone in his circle) before he
came across Einhard's book; and then underwent successive
revisions, as it was gradually assimilated to its model. In
this connexion one recalls Wanley's assertion that the
Cottonian MS 'was not written by one hand, but by
several and much about the same time'. This is an odd
feature in so small a book and suggests that the Cotton
MS may have been no more than a much-altered draft of a
work that was finished, but never finally revised.

Bishop Leofric, as a Welshman or more probably a
Cornishman, can be reasonably credited, like Nennius
before him, with 'a patriotic heart'[1] despite his continental
education. Nennius had addressed his book to the Cymric
people, including Cambrians, but the author of 'Asser'
was of necessity writing for all England. His main purpose
was to idealise King Alfred, but he was only less concerned
to glorify Asser, whose life and fortunes he sets out in
imaginary detail and at undue length. His reason for
halting the Life in the year 893 can only be guessed at. He
may have realised that he did not know enough of Alfred's
literary labours—who did in the eleventh century?—to
finish the book. More certainly, the prominence given to
bishop Asser seems to be connected with transference of
his Devonshire see to Exeter and the final suppression of
the separate Cornish bishopric. In the eleventh century
nothing was known of Asser except that he had helped
Alfred with his translations and that he had died in 910 as
bishop of Sherborne. When he was appointed was not
known; and since nowhere in the Life is he so referred to,

[1] See Liebermann's essay on Nennius in *Essays presented to T. F. Tout*
(1925), p. 43. Although the author of 'Asser' makes a show of speaking 'of
England and the English *as if* he were addressing his own countrymen' the
book is really designed for an English audience, and in c. 79, l. 1–3, he
clearly thinks of St David's as 'at the back of beyond'.

the author may well have stopped at the year 893 to avoid
the double dilemma of his ignorance of Alfred's translations and the date of Asser's advancement to Sherborne.
The choice of the year 893 excused any mention of most of
the translations, and left time for Asser to have become
bishop of Sherborne before the king's death in 899.

It remains to remind ourselves of the uncovenanted
advantages conferred by the hypothesis of an eleventh-
century author. A whole series of 'difficulties' which
Stevenson strove to answer in his Notes are more simply
explained by the later date of composition. The em-
broideries of his translation of the Chronicle read more
like the glosses of a late translator than genuine additions
to knowledge made by a contemporary. The use of *rex
Angulsaxonum* as the royal style points to the later date
when, as Stevenson points out, it was popular with would-
be archaic writers. The credit of the author has no longer
to be saved by translating *Wintonia* as Winchester in c. 18
and Caerwent in c. 79. The allusions to Oslac, the famous
*pincerna* of Aethelwulf (c. 2), and to Offa's Dyke (c. 14)
surely find their spiritual home in the eleventh, rather than
the ninth century, as does the fluent continental Latin in
which the book is written. The concise synthesis of Welsh
history in Alfred's reign (c. 80) must surely have been
beyond the mental grasp of a contemporary Welshman,
and is better referred to the eleventh century. The stories,
too, belong to folklore and legend—Alfred as a child
reading the book, the story of Eadburh and Charlemagne,
the incredible account of Alfred threatening to dismiss his
thegns and magistrates from office unless they applied
themselves to learning and of their frantic efforts to com-
ply, the business of the candles and the horn lantern—all
these are of the same vintage as Alfred and the Cakes which

we know to belong to the eleventh century. Of c. 106,[1] the description of Alfred's justice, it is sufficient to observe that it has not been called into service by our legal historians; while the avidity with which the makers of forged charters in the eleventh and twelfth centuries turned to the Life has had the curious effect of making Stevenson's book the *locus classicus* for the study of forgery in that period.

One can readily understand the reluctance of experts to jettison what they consider to be a key document for the chronology of Alfred's reign; but it requires the faith that moves mountains to accept the Life as the work of an educated ecclesiastic who had lived in Alfred's household and who had 'looked upon his face'. The more intimate passages, which invoke the miraculous, belong almost to hagiography; but Alfred was never a candidate for sanctity in his lifetime, though not far removed from it by some eleventh-century writers. It lacks both the humour and the immediacy which belong to contemporary writing. Yet it preserves much sober historical truth and more valuable tradition; and, taken as a whole, it stands midway between the historical Alfred of the Chronicle and the translations, and the purely legendary figure of the later Middle Ages.

How far has this paper complied with the principles of criticism mentioned above?[2]

So far as concerns No. 1 there has been no great difficulty, because the problem was a simple choice between

---

[1] Stevenson considered that this chapter raised 'serious difficulties' but Professor Whitelock (p. cxlvii of the reprint of Stevenson) argues that there is nothing in it to warrant the suspicion with which it has been regarded.

[2] p. 87.

the only two possible alternatives. We have, no doubt, gone beyond the limits of strict demonstration in suggesting a definite author for the work, but the argument for an eleventh-century date stands upon the solid foundation of the actual text of the Life. Despite many differences of interpretation the argument rests upon Stevenson's own premises, and has in fact done no more than carry his 'unsolved' difficulties to their logical conclusion.

The real problem has lain in adhering to our second principle, viz. to make our scrutiny objective and impartial. It will have been obvious to the reader that it has proved impossible to be entirely objective, since the whole inquiry arose from the subjective impression gained from the first reading of the book. One has been driven into the position of an advocate of the later date of composition— a sort of counsel for the prosecution. However deplorable, this appears to be unavoidable; and I am confirmed in this view by the conviction derived from studying Stevenson's evidence over many years. Stevenson, despite every effort to act as a just judge between the two alternatives, was equally the victim of his underlying feeling in favour of the earlier date. On a close reading he appears as, in fact, counsel for the defence,[1] pouring scorn for example on T. E. Wright,[2] who attacked the date, before he even mentions his views, and 'explaining' the silence of

---

[1] The same is true of Professor Whitelock. See her able summary of recent work on Asser in the reprint of the Life (1959). Professor Whitelock, if I understand her aright, finds no 'difficulties' in Asser, and unhesitatingly endorses Stevenson's conclusions.

[2] p. xcvi: 'In 1841 Thomas Wright, who about this period was strenuously defending the authenticity of the absurd forgery De situ Britanniae, which Bartram fathered upon Richard of Cirencester, communicated to the Society of Antiquaries a paper in which he threw doubts upon the authenticity of the Life.' Cf. also p. 108, n. 2 above, and p. 126 below.

Aethelweard in a disingenuous as well as an inaccurate manner. To Stevenson 'forgery' implied a criminal offence, and nowhere does the alternative of late composition receive an impartial assessment. This pervading difficulty in the criticism of literary texts appears to me to be almost insoluble, except perhaps by stating all the pros and cons in intolerable and unpractical detail.

The moral of all this seems to be that in questions involving literary texts, the element of personal feeling—the purely subjective judgment—is not merely unavoidable, but necessary, and in some cases all-important. Following Stevenson, I have treated the Life in isolation, as just another history or biography. But quite obviously it is both more and less than either, and it would be of interest to try to recreate the background reading and outlook of the author. Professor Southern believes that whoever wrote it was deeply versed in the writings of the Desert Fathers; and he may well be right, for in more than one passage there is a strain of devotion and contemplation foreign to the basic pattern imposed by the translation of the Chronicle. However that may be, there certainly runs through it a hagiographical strain reminiscent of a wide category of medieval writings—the lives of the Saints. These seem to use earlier documents. Sometimes authentic material can be disinterred, though this is a ticklish business, and the mere fact that a saint's life may get the topography right is no evidence of anything save the hagiographer's familiarity with the places he is writing about. Hagiographers tend to be naïve, to deal in types rather than individuals and to repeat monotonously the same miracles and traits of a great number of Saints. Asser, of course, is less stylised than the hagiographers, and uses much good historical material. Yet through it runs a thread of near-hagiography, exhibiting most of the above traits.

Within this large category fall, too, those apocryphal Gospels and Acts which comprise the Apocryphal New Testament.[1] These do not provide direct parallels, of course, but do at least illustrate how uninhibited and fertile in creation the authors of apocryphal documents could be. M. R. James, in his handy edition of the Apocryphal New Testament, faces the charge that the New Testament is an arbitrary selection made by the early fathers from a great mass of Acts, Gospels, and so on. But his reply is '—Read them and you will see that the false gospels are not excluded—they exclude themselves'. In them the same characteristics re-appear again and again. The authors are anxious to increase faith and add to the meagre survivals from the past. They show, like Asser, a concern about one special virtue, the virtue of chastity. They everywhere claim to first-hand authority: the authors either took part in the events they describe or can quote the very words of the Master. *Mutatis mutandis*, all this is equally true of Asser, or, as I would now call him, the pseudo-Asser, though the interval is shorter and the historical material more copious. Yet he excludes himself from true history; and he does so, not so much by his anachronisms, as by his pervasive quality of excessive naïvety. One form of this naïvety lies in his recurrent exaggeration which often borders upon absurdity: another (especially evident in cc. 79–81 and cc. 88–9) lies in an excess of trivial, personal details, coupled with inevitable

[1] *The Apocryphal New Testament*, ed. by M. R. James (Clarendon Press, 1960). I am grateful to Professor Henry Chadwick for introducing me to this book, and for instruction in its use: but he bears no responsibility for what is said above.

vagueness regarding what should be hard facts: and still another in plain childishness, as when he explains the general reluctance to enter the cloister as due to *either* the Danish invasions *or* the abundance of every sort of riches— *nescio quare*—he does not know which.

These analogies did not entirely escape Stevenson, who at the close of his long Introduction listed the unsolved 'difficulties' with which the *Life* had confronted him.

But when all his foreign matter has been excised [he wrote], the work still presents some difficulties. Carelessness of transcription may possibly explain those that are merely verbal, but there still remain certain passages that lay the author open to the charge of exaggeration, such as his mention of gold-covered and silver-covered buildings (c. 91. 20), if that be the literal meaning of the passage, and his statement that Alfred might if he had chosen, have been king before his elder brother Aethelred (c. 42. 6), with whom, it is clear, he was on most intimate terms. The account of Alfred's early illness, of his cure, of his praying for an infirmity that should keep him in the paths of chastity, of the cure of the illness thus acquired at his marriage, and of his being then stricken with a compensatory infirmity immediately afterwards (c. 74) are hard to believe literally. The morbid feelings here described to the king read more like a chapter from a saint's life. . . .

Stevenson then attempts to explain this chapter rationally and historically as due to the author's love of rhetoric which led him into exaggeration either for the purposes of 'heightening the colours of his picture, or of emphasising the difficulties under which the king performed his life's strenuous work'.

But in either case [he adds] the result must be to shake our confidence in his strict veracity.

And concludes with the passage 'Much may be forgiven . . .' already quoted above (p. 89). In this long and revealing quotation we see Stevenson vainly seeking to treat as actual some of the hagiographical elements in the Life, which really lie outside the historical field. They are un-mistakable and are characterised by the excessive naïvety which pervades so much of the narrative, and give the lie to its claim to be contemporary.

The same failure to grasp the nature of his material is equally apparent in Stevenson's treatment of the merely traditional and legendary elements in the Life. It is full of the folklore that grows around the memory of a great man, and the long note on pp. 339-40 discussing (with a large apparatus of classical learning) whether Alfred really *was* the inventor of the horn lantern (c. 104) is surely an instance of a non-existent mountain in labour producing an imaginary mouse.

It would seem [writes Stevenson] that it was the planning of the lantern, not the use of it to shield his time-candles from the wind, that the author ascribes to Alfred, but his style is so involved and his thoughts generally so confused that it is conceivable that he meant merely that Alfred applied the lantern to this purpose.

Here, as so often, Stevenson from sheer lack of under-standing is unfair to this author, who had a good story to tell and, however naïvely, told it. There are, in short, limits to the possibilities of the dead hand of sheer learning, and even if some of the 'difficulties' discussed above should by some fortunate chance be cleared up, we should still have to hesitate before accepting 'Asser' as a genuine ninth-century Life.

The intensive study of Anglo-Saxon history in the past century has posed a difficulty for all who today attempt a rounded portrait of King Alfred. In the Chronicle we have the stark picture of the indomitable warrior, so vivid as to suggest that the narrative of his reign, if hardly of his early years, was strictly contemporary. Scholars have also drawn from the translations a clear impression of Alfred's interest in the eternal problems of life and death, of fate and free will, unique in the whole line of our early kings. Between these two pictures there is a superficial paradox, or at least a conjunction of qualities sufficiently rare to demand explanation. This difficulty must have been already dimly felt in the eleventh century, when the victories of Alfred's successors and their final eclipse in the renewed Danish invasions had given rise to an undergrowth of tradition, legend, and folk memory of every sort and kind. Alfred's fame—one might almost say his cult—grew steadily; there was by this time a popular assurance of his greatness, and he was now seen as comparable in achievement with Charles the Great. This analogy was seized upon by 'Asser'; and in the Life he strove to bridge the gap between the scholar and the warrior by making Alfred's ninth-century Welsh helper the author of an English 'Einhard'. For all its faults the Life was a creditable piece of historical research: far superior, for example, to Geoffrey of Monmouth's later attempt at early history. It is informed by a real, if limited, historical sense, and its literary sources would still repay examination. The author's curiosity reaches back far beyond Alfred to the beginnings of the Anglo-Saxons. He quotes Sedulius, and is interested in King Offa, and in his famous Dyke. He is something, too, of a geographer, and a student of philology, and not un-aware of continental history. By and large, he is not un-representative of the intellectual movement of the eleventh century, and his book may well have been known to the author of the *Encomium Emmae*. The Life, moreover, is in its way an imaginative book, though the great king is still

seen through a glass darkly, owing to the recurrent hagio-
graphic strain that runs through it. It describes the warrior,
and it describes the near-saint, without fusing the two men
into a living picture. His Alfred smacks rather of the
cloister, and we have to wait till the next century for the
firmer and more credible portrait of William of Malmesbury. This was due to his wider scholarship and to the fact
that he himself never encountered the Life. He knew it
only from the chronicle of Florence of Worcester, from
which he borrowed freely, but—with a sure instinct—
'played down' the neurotic passages in his source. His
picture marks the high point in medieval understanding of
the King, and even the best of later accounts merely repeat
his words.

It is thus a matter of some importance to have rescued
Alfred from the charge of having been a *malade imaginaire*,
and to see him again as the simple, great-hearted warrior
he was. There can still be two opinions as to whether it was
Leofric who wrote the Life. But the discussion of this
narrower problem has at least shown that the author of the
Life lived more than a century after Alfred's death.

# GLOSSARY

ANGLO-NORMAN FRENCH The particular French dialect developed in England after the Norman Conquest. It produced a literature of its own and lasted for four centuries.

ARCHIVES Ordinary business records put away for reference. They are thus 'dead' papers which reflect the structure and working of the organisation which produced them.

AULNAGE, ULNAGE Duty on cloth. The ulnager was the official who affixed his seal to the cloths thus making them current merchandise.

BULLS (PAPAL) The *bulla* was the pendent, leaden seal which authenticated papal letters. By association the letters acquired the name of 'papal bulls'.

CAROLINE MINUSCULE Early Latin scripts are conventionally divided into two branches, the majuscule and the minuscule. The former includes four types, viz. square capitals, rustic capitals, uncial and half-uncial. Of these, uncials and half-uncials were in common use for some centuries after the break up of the Roman Empire. From the early eighth century there arose a number of local scripts, the chief of which was the Caroline minuscule, described by E. A. Lowe as 'the medieval contribution to writing *par excellence*'. First taken up at the court of the emperor Charles the Great, it gradually penetrated into England for Latin manuscripts, though books in the vernacular continued to be written in the native, 'insular', minuscule. All these scripts were 'bookhands', that is scripts appropriate for works of lasting value.

CHANCERY The royal secretariat, presided over by the King's Chancellor, who was the *ex officio* Keeper of the Great Seal.

CHANCERY ENROLMENTS The Chancery rolls contain copies of out-letters under the great seal. The roll was made up of parchment membranes, sewn together end to end. The chief classes were the Charter, Patent, Close and Fine Rolls, of which the Patent and Close Rolls continue to this day. Both sides of the parchment were normally written on. They are cumbrous to use as the whole roll—

twenty feet or more—may have to be unrolled to find a particular entry.

CHARTERS The word charter is commonly used to denote any form of deed or conveyance, but the term was reserved in the royal Chancery for important grants made in perpetuity.

CHIROGRAPH The earliest form of indenture or charter-party. Two (or three) copies of a document were written on a single sheet of parchment, divided by the word CYROGRAPHUM in large capital letters. The sheet was then cut through this word, thus producing two (or three) authentic copies.

CONSTABLE A term applied to many officials in the Middle Ages. The king's household had its constable, and there were constables of castles, hundreds and of villages. The village constable survived until the creation of the modern police force in the nineteenth century.

COURT HAND The cursive script of business documents and of everyday life, as opposed to Text or Bookhand.

COURT ROLL The records of the proceedings of most courts of law were formerly kept on parchment rolls; but the term is generally restricted to the record of the court of the manor or estate. The manorial court was normally held by the lord's steward, and, according to the lawyers, met in three capacities—the Court Baron for freeholders, the Court Custumary for copy-holders, and the Court Leet, which was concerned with keeping the king's peace within the manor.

CURSIVE All writing may be broadly divided into Text or Bookhand, and Cursive. From the latter emerged Court Hand, a script suitable for administrative and official documents.

DIPLOMATIC The barbarous name given to the science of documents. It is borrowed from the French *Diplomatique*, who took it from Mabillon's *De re diplomatica* (1681). In classical Rome a diploma was a two-leaved letter of recommendation, or passport.

DONATION OF CONSTANTINE A document concocted in the early Middle Ages by which the emperor Constantine bestowed on the Pope and his successors sovereignty over Italy and the countries of the west. It is described by Bryce as 'the most stupendous of all medieval forgeries, which for seven centuries commanded the almost unquestioning belief of mankind'. It was shown to be a forgery by Lorenzo Valla, a fifteenth-century humanist.

EXCHEQUER The financial department of the government. The Exchequer was divided into the Upper Exchequer, which was simply the *curia regis* sitting for the regulation of finance, and the Lower Exchequer or accounting department of the royal Treasury. The term Exchequer (or chess board) refers to the system of accounting by the use of the abacus.

FINE A fictitious suit by which an absolute title was established upon land. A Fine (i.e. a final agreement) was said to be 'levied'.

GOTHIC SCRIPT The name given by the Humanists to the angular bookhand which dominated European writing from the thirteenth to the fifteenth centuries. It is still to be seen on many monumental brasses of the period.

HALF-UNCIAL An early medieval script. *See* CAROLINE MINUSCULE.

INDENTURE or charter party. Two copies of a document on a single sheet, cut through in a series of indentations to produce two counterparts.

INQUISITION POST MORTEM The inquisition or inquest was the normal means of collecting information used by the Crown. Inquisitions *post mortem* were taken by the sheriff who committed to writing the sworn declaration of the jury regarding the lands of a deceased tenant in chief.

LETTER CLOSE A writ or letter which was closed by the seal. To read it, the seal had to be broken.

LETTER PATENT An open writ or letter from which the seal depended.

MANOR The word was used vaguely to signify a landed estate. By the thirteenth century it came to imply the existence of a manorial court held by the lord of the manor.

MEMBRANE *See* PARCHMENT.

MISERICORD A projection, often carved, on the underside of a stall seat, which gave support when the seat was turned up.

NOTARY A professional scribe. There were two kinds of notaries, those who acted by imperial, and those who acted by papal authority. They were much used for making certified copies of important documents. Each notary had his own distinctive mark.

OPEN FIELD Medieval agriculture was based upon either the two-field or the three-field system, by which the arable was divided into two or three open fields, one of which was fallow.

PALAEOGRAPHY The name given to the study of hand-writing. The word comes from the Greek, and means simply old writing.

PAPER The normal material for writing and printing since the fifteenth century. It seems to have originated in China, and was introduced into Europe by the Arabs. A knowledge of the water-marks of different periods is necessary to date paper manuscripts.

PAPYRUS The normal writing material of classical Greece and Rome, made from a plant cultivated in the Delta of Egypt.

PARCHMENT The normal writing material from about the fourth century A.D., when it superseded papyrus, until the later Middle Ages, when it was in turn superseded by paper. Parchment is made from the skins of sheep, goats or calves. The finer qualities, made from the skins of still-born calves, were called *vellum*, and this word is now indiscriminately employed without warrant in describing manuscripts. When rolls are referred to, each sheet of parchment is called a 'membrane' (Latin: *membrana*, a skin). The word parchment ultimately derives from Pergamum in Mysia, traditionally the town in which it originated.

PIPE ROLL The common name for the annual 'great roll' of the Exchequer, made up once a year at Michaelmas. The earliest surviving specimen is that of 31 Henry I, and they are more or less complete from 2 Henry II until the year 1834, when they came to an end. Pipe rolls consisted of a number of membranes gathered at the head, and each membrane, made up of two skins sewn together, was technically a 'pipe'.

PLEA ROLL There were two great series of plea rolls, those of the Court of King's Bench (*coram rege*) and those of the Court of Common Pleas (*de banco*). Unlike the rolls of Chancery, each roll consisted of a large number of membranes gathered at the head.

PRIVY SEAL The king's privy seal first appears in the early thir-teenth century as the special seal of the king's household. It gave rise to a second, royal secretariat the head of which survives today as a cabinet officer, though his seal was abolished a century ago.

RECOVERY A fictitious suit in the Court of Common Pleas by which a tenant secured a better title to his land. He was said to 'suffer a Recovery'.

ROLLS OF PARLIAMENT Household records made by the king's clerks from the reign of Edward I. In the following century the record of the doings of Parliament became the duty of the king's

Chancery. They were published by the Record Commission in six volumes, with a fine index (1832).

RUSTIC CAPITALS An early majuscule script. *See* CAROLINE MINUSCULE.

SCRIVENERS Public writers of the 'court letter' or Court Hand organised in town guilds or companies. The Common Paper of the London company in which each Master made his autograph entry survives from the fourteenth century onwards. There are facsimiles of these entries in Hilary Jenkinson's *Later Court Hands in England* (1927).

SEISIN Seisin means possession as distinct from ownership. In the Middle Ages transfers of land were normally completed by a formal 'livery' (i.e. delivery) 'of seisin'.

SIGNET A signet ring. In the fourteenth century a third royal secretariat arose, presided over by the King's Secretary, who kept his signet. This official was the lineal ancestor of the heads of the chief modern government departments. The Signet Office was abolished in the nineteenth century.

STATE PAPERS The name first given to the records of the king's two Principal Secretaries in the reign of Henry VIII. The State Paper Office was established by Queen Elizabeth in 1578. The immense bulk of its records are still being printed in summary form by the Public Record Office in its *Calendars of State Papers*.

TALLY A notched stick used in accounting. The sum of money involved was shown by the notches cut in the stick which was then cut through longitudinally, thus producing two identical receipts. (See Plate XI.)

TENANT IN CHIEF A landowner who held his land directly from the king.

UNCIAL An early majuscule script. *See* CAROLINE MINUSCULE.

VELLUM *See* PARCHMENT.

VESTRY The meeting of the inhabitants of a parish. The name first comes into use in the sixteenth century.

# NOTES ON THE TEXT

1. E. L. Woodward, *War and peace in Europe* 1815–1870 (Constable, 1931), pp. 119–176  *page* 18

2. R. W. Southern, *The shape and substance of academic history* (O.U.P., 1961)  *page* 20

3. R. G. Collingwood and J. N. Myres, *Roman Britain and the English settlements* (O.U.P., 1936), pp. 325–456  *page* 31

4. W. A. Pantin, *Monuments or muniments?* (Medieval Archaeology, Vol. II, 1958)  *page* 31

5. W. E. Tate, *The parish chest* (C.U.P., 1946), p. 67 which analyses the relevant material  *page* 36

6. The date has since been extended to include selected monuments up to the middle of the nineteenth century  *page* 38

7. J. Summerson, *Georgian London* (Pleiades Books, 1945), p. 126  *page* 39

8. D. Piper, *The English face* (Thames and Hudson, 1957), Chapter XIV  *page* 46

9. B. H. St J. O'Neil, *Castles and cannon* (O.U.P., 1960)  *page* 46

10. E. Carus-Wilson, *Medieval merchant venturers* (Methuen, 1954), p. 291  *page* 53

# SOME BOOKS FOR FURTHER READING

*not mentioned in the text*

## Original sources

ALL understanding of the past ultimately depends upon the study of the original sources, which, of course, include the whole of the literature and records of one's chosen period. For the modern period the *World's Classics* and *Everyman's Library* offer a wide selection of texts. The Middle Ages, for which most of the contemporary material is in Latin, French or Old English, are less well served, though there is an excellent edition of the *Anglo-Saxon Chronicle* (ed. Garmonsway) and a translation of Bede's *Ecclesiastical History* in the *Everyman* series. A selection of medieval books in translation is also published in the *King's Classics* (Chatto & Windus), while Nelson's *Medieval Texts* provide both the Latin text and a translation of more than a score of historical books. The massive *English Historical Documents*, 7 volumes, under the general editorship of Professor Douglas, will when complete provide a large *corpus* of medieval and modern source material in translation. So far only volumes I, II, VIII, X and XI have appeared.

## General

BLOCH, M. *The historian's craft* Manchester U.P., 1954. 12s 6d

CARR, E. H. *What is history?* Macmillan, 1961. 21s

COLLINGWOOD, R. G. *The idea of history* O.U.P., 1946. 28s

CRUMP, C. G. *History and historical research* Routledge, 1928

ENSOR, R. C. K. and others *Why we study history* Historical Association, No. 131. 1944

GRETTON, R. H. *History (Art and craft of letters)* Secker, 1914

LYNAM, E. *British maps and mapmakers (Britain in pictures)* Collins, 1944

MARTIN, C. T. *The record interpreter: a collection of abbreviations, Latin words, and names used in English historical manuscripts and records* Sweet & Maxwell, 2nd edn. 1910. 35s

NEVINS, A. *The gateway to history* D. M. Heath, 1938
WEAVER, F. J. *The material of English history. (Discussion books, No. 10)* Nelson, 1938. 2s

## The Public Record Office

GALBRAITH, V. H. *Introduction to the use of public records* O.U.P., 1934. 8s 6d
GALBRAITH, V. H. *Studies in the public records* Nelson, 1948. 6s

## Palaeography

CAPPELLI, A. *Dizionario de abbreviatore Latine e Italiane* Milan: Hoepli, 1912
ESSEX COUNTY RECORD OFFICE *Examples of English handwriting, 1150–1750; by H. E. P. Grieve* Chelmsford: Essex C.C., 2nd edn. 1959. 12s 6d
HECTOR, L. C. *The handwriting of English documents* Arnold, 1958. 30s
HECTOR, L. C. *Palaeography and forgery* St Anthony's Press, 1959. 3s 6d
THOMPSON, SIR E. M. *An introduction to Greek and Latin palaeography* (the standard book of reference) O.U.P., 1912

## Local Records

EMMISON, F. G. and GRAY, I. *County records (Helps for students of history, H.62)* Historical Assoc., 2nd edn. 1961. 5s
FINBERG, H. P. R. *The local historian and his theme. (Leicester Univ. College, Dept. of Local History, Occasional Papers, No. 1)* Leicester: University College; 1952. 3s
PUGH, R. *How to write a parish history* Allen & Unwin, 1954. 8s 6d
TATE, W. E. *The parish chest* C.U.P., 1946. 35s

## Chronology

CHENEY, C. R. *Handbook of dates for students of English history.* Royal Historical Soc., 2nd edn. 1955. 12s 6d

*Allied subjects*

BETJEMAN, J. ed. *Collins guide to English parish churches* Collins, 1958. 30s

BRITISH MUSEUM *A guide to the British Museum* The Trustees of the Museum. 2s 6d

BROOKE, G. C. *English coins from the seventh century to the present day* (the standard book of reference) Methuen, 3rd edn. 1950. 45s

BROWN, R. A. *English mediaeval castles* Batsford, 1954. 16s

CRUDEN, S. *The Scottish castle* (*Studies in history and archaeology*) Nelson, 1960. 42s

FAIRBANK, A. *A book of scripts* Penguin Books, 1949. 5s

KNOWLES, D. and ST JOSEPH, J. K. S. *Monastic sites from the air* C.U.P., 1952. 55s

MILNE, J. G. and others *Coin collecting* O.U.P., 1950. 12s 6d

MINISTRY OF WORKS *Scottish Abbeys: an introd. to the mediaeval abbeys and priories of Scotland, by S. Cruden* Edinburgh: H.M.S.O., 1960. 7s 6d

PIGGOTT, STUART. *Approach to Archaeology* Adam and Charles Black, 1959. 15s

POOLE, A. L. ed. *Mediaeval England* (an authoritative survey of every aspect of medieval history) O.U.P., 2nd edn. 1958. 2 vols. 70s

PUBLIC RECORD OFFICE *A guide to the seals in the Public Record Office* H.M.S.O., 1954. 4s

RICHARDS, J. M. *A miniature history of the English house* Architectural P., 2nd edn. 1950. 6s

WAGNER, A. R. *Heraldry in England* Penguin Books, 1946

WAGNER, A. R. *English ancestry* (*Oxford paperbacks*) O.U.P., 1961. 6s

WYON, A. B. and A. *The great seals of England* (the standard book of reference) Stock, 1887

THE HISTORICAL ASSOCIATION (59A Kennington Park Road, S.E.11) exists to further the study of History and membership is open to all interested in the subject. The Association publishes many valuable pamphlets, issued at reduced rates to members. It has also continued the invaluable *Helps for students of history*, originally published by the S.P.C.K. Many of these, though now out of print, can be picked up second hand. Among the most useful are the following:

CRUMP, C. G. *The logic of history (Helps for students of history No. 6)* S.P.C.K., 1919. 8d

JOHNSON, C. *The mechanical processes of the historian (Helps for students of history No. 50)* S.P.C.K., 1922. 6d

JOHNSON, C. *The Public Record Office (Helps for students of history No. 4)* S.P.C.K., 1918. 6d

KINGSFORD, H. S. *Seals (Helps for students of history No. 30)* S.P.C.K., 1921. 1s 3d

MARSHALL, R. L. *Historical criticism of documents (Helps for students of history, No. 28)* S.P.C.K., 1920. 1s 3d

POOLE, R. L. *Mediaeval reckonings of time (Helps for students of history No. 3)* S.P.C.K., 1918. 6d

# INDEX

Acton, Lord (1834–1902), 13
Adam, the first man, 36
Additional Manuscripts (B.M.), 54
Aerial photography, 7, 137
Aethelred I, K. of Wessex, brother of K. Alfred, 93, 121, 125
Aethelweard, chronicle of, 89, 108
Alfred, K. of the West Saxons: Life of, described, 88, 99; only MS destroyed, 88; its date, 94; problem of authorship, 88–91; anachronisms in, 91–7; Dedication to Alfred, 91, 116–17; hypothesis of Leofric's authorship, 99–103, 117–18; author's revision of his text, 111–16; advantages of the later date, 120; excessive naïvety of the Life, 123–5; value of the Life, 126–8
'Alfred and the Cakes', 87, 120
Anderson, M. D., 47
Anglo-Saxon Chronicle, 102, 118; basis of the Life of Alfred, 85, 86, 89, 90; mistranslated in the Life, 91, 92
*Angulsaxonum Rex*, title discussed, 92, 93, 120
Anne, Q. of Richard II, 72
Apocryphal New Testament, 124
Archaeology, 30–2
Archaeology, Council for British, 31
Archaeology, Society of Medieval, 31
Architecture and building, 38–40
Archives, National Register of, 55
Arnold, Thomas (1795–1842), 76–77

Asser, B. of Sherborne, 85, 88, 104; one of Alfred's helpers, 85, 98; 101; died in 910, 85; not called B. of Sherborne in the Life, 98; fictitious autobiography of, 104

Banwell, Somerset, 95, 97, 98
Bayeux Tapestry, 36
Bede, the Venerable, 26, 31; translation of, 102
Bentley, Richard (1662–1742), 16
Bigot, Roger, 67
Bloch, Marc (1886–1944), 3
Bodleian Library, 49
Boethius' *Consolation of Philosophy*, 101, 102
Bouwen, B. G., 45
Bresslau, Harry, 25
British Museum, 24, 49, 54–5
British Records Association, 48
Bury, J. B. (1861–1927), 3, 59, 60
Butterfield, Herbert, 6

Caerwent, Monmouth, 98, 120
Caistor next Norwich, 70
Calne, Wilts, 67
Cambridge, city of, 39
*Cambridge Modern History*, 74
Cambridge University Library, 49
Cameron, Kenneth, 38
Campbell, Alistair, 89, 108
Canterbury, archbishopric of, 15
Canterbury, Prerogative Court of, 45
Carlyle, Thomas (1795–1881), 20
Caroline minuscule, 22, 66, 129
Carus-Wilson, Eleanora, 53
Cerdic, 36
Chadwick, Henry, 124
Chancellor, the king's, 7, 40, 51, 129